SHEARSMAN

117 & 118

WINTER 2018 / 2019

GUEST EDITOR, 117/118
KELVIN CORCORAN

EDITOR
TONY FRAZER

Shearsman magazine is published in the United Kingdom by
Shearsman Books Ltd
50 Westons Hill Drive
Emersons Green
BRISTOL   BS16 7DF

Registered office: 30-31 St James Place, Mangotsfield, Bristol BS16 9JB
(this address not for correspondence)

www. shearsman.com

ISBN 978-1-84861-603-5
ISSN 0260-8049

Subscriptions and single copies

Current subscriptions – covering two double-issues, each around 100 pages in length
– cost £16 for delivery to U.K. addresses, £18 for the rest of Europe (including the
Republic of Ireland), and £22 for the rest of the world. Longer subscriptions may
be had for a pro-rata higher payment. Purchasers from North America will find that
buying single copies from online retailers in the U.S.A. or Canada will be cheaper
than subscribing. This is because airmail postage rates in the U.K. have risen rapidly,
whereas copies of the magazine are printed in the U.S.A. to meet orders from online
retailers there, and thus avoid the costly transatlantic mail.

Back issues from n° 63 onwards (uniform with this issue) cost £8.95 / $16 through
retail outlets. Single copies can be ordered for £8.95 direct from the press, post-free
within the U.K., through the Shearsman Books online store, or from bookshops.
Issues of the previous pamphlet-style version of the magazine, from n° 1 to n° 62,
may be had for £3 each, direct from the press, where copies are still available, but
contact us for a quote for a full, or partial, run.

Submissions

Shearsman operates a submissions-window system, whereby submissions may only
be made during the months of March and September, when selections are made for
the October and April issues, respectively. Submissions may be sent by mail or email,
but email attachments are only accepted in PDF form. We aim to respond within 3
months of the window's closure, i.e. all who submit *should* hear by the end of June
or December, although for recent issues we have sometimes taken a little longer.

This issue has been set in Bembo with titling in Argumentum.
The flyleaf is set in Trend Sans.

Contents

Lance Nizami   5
Cathy Dreyer   10
Hilda Sheehan   14
Jill Jones   18
Drew Milne   25
Khaled Hakim   29
Barbara Tomash   33
Janet Sutherland   35
Martin Corless-Smith   41
Carrie Etter   46
Robert Sheppard   49
Tamar Yoseloff   51
James Bell   52
Martin Anderson   57
Susie Campbell   66
Natasha Sajé   69
Lucy Sheerman   72
Julie Mellor   74
Gillian Kidd Osborne   77
Ralph Hawkins   81
Guy Birchard   85

Judita Vaičiūnaitė   89
Giedrė Kazlauskaitė   94
Indrė Valantinaitė   97
(translated from Lithuanian by Rimas Uzgiris)

Notes on Contributors   100

Lance Nizami

Observance

A mountain town: in-deep the valley in-between the hazy Sawtooth
    peaks
An inn; the far-north-side of town
A room that faces north, too, with a balcony
And there we sit and eat, late sunbathed autumn afternoon

The Chinese food is good here, unexpected in this mountain town
The hillsides golden-grassed between the pines are dry and dusty
So, too, the air; each moisture-molecule is bound to dust
Below us, close nearby, the one exception: grass that's green and wet
    and trimmed

The cemetery; stretching northwards, linear, road-side; cemetery
Inside, a lone black road, well-paved, loops in, then out of graveyard
And as we watch, a ritual unfolds:

A car rolls in; it stops along the right-hand-side of tarmac, though no
    markings are apparent
The doors will open; grown-ups exit, kids are left behind to wait
Grown-ups walk short-ways, in silence; disappear, in conifers
And then: no motion

Grown-ups then trace their steps back to their vehicle
They step inside, the doors close, and they leave –
A minute passes, sometimes two; and then a different car appears, or
    sometimes two
Then debarkation, walk, and pause; then embarkation, drive away

The minutes pass; the ritual repeats
As dusk approaches, cars decline in frequency
We sit and watch, few words between us, waiting –
And finally, our greed for food is sated and our greed to know
    breaks free –

We walk downstairs; across the moist green grass; along the tarmac
We estimate the spot where others stopped their vehicles
We turn, and walk across wet grass in lessening autumn light
And there's the grove of trees, the conifers

A gap between the pines leaves room for two flat slabs of greying
      granite
Side-by-side; a man, and final wife
And on the husband's slab, we see an unexpected scattering:
Coins and plastic pens, and one lone paper note: it's "Thank You"

A name's carved deep upon the greying slab:
ERNEST MILLER HEMINGWAY
And suddenly, we comprehend the ritual
And suddenly, we're cast into a silence

And now we know why cars will stop here, next day and the next
And now we sense that we, like others, realize the place's meaning
Pausing, remembering –

Hemingway; his novels, read in high-school class; we had no choice
And later, when we wrote, we understood that obligation
And here, in this dark grove, we now recall:
An aging Cuban fights for hours against the vicious sharks, to keep
      a massive tuna-fish, and fails

He fails; his tears add salt to salty water
And here, beneath the conifers, our unexpected tears add salt to soil
In a mountain town, so far from sandy shores of far-off Cuba
A mountain town: in-deep the valley in-between the hazy Sawtooth
      peaks.

Drive

Speed
The edges blur, the center sharpens
I feel the air as things recede from me
I feel vibrations underneath my seat
My right foot, rigid, holds against the pedal
My right hand grips the wheel, with rigid force
My left hand sits with lightness on the shifter
Speed

Speed
I cannot live without it
I cannot see how anybody can
To make the world pass quickly by is glorious
I sweat as the adrenaline floods through me
My hands are wet inside my leather gloves
My shoulders stiffen, with acceleration
Speed

Speed
God Almighty, if I live I'll shout, exult –
The only way to live is live like this
I dread the day I ever pause too long
I fear I'll lose my nerve and not return
We keep our nerve by moving always moving
It's in our blood; we have the need for more and more of
Speed

Speed
And everything we do acquires momentum
Momentum – moving, one task to the next
Everything we do starts from momentum
Momentum is the muscle of our action
It's vector is velocity, it's magnitude is mass
Direction? dashed white line will show the needed way of
Speed

Speed
The vector changes, maybe; never drops to zero
Our lives are all trajectories, none straight
Tires screaming, at the corners, we will push our bodies' limits
We'll push the limits of our very minds
We'll feel the air as things recede from us
The edges blur, the center sharpens
Speed

Stockton Street, SF, June

The stained streets and the hardness of concrete under my hard-soled boots and the old short Chinese hobbling with canes and the smell of vegetables and the stark advent of sunlight and the cool dark shade of alleyways and the crowded sidewalk and the babble of voices and the occasional blare of automobile horns and the occasional squeals of circling children and the vans unloading streetside and the utter clear blueness of the sky and the lurid reds and yellows of storefront signs and the gold and white and brown and green and synthetic day-glo pink of clothes in windows and the sudden welcome breeze-brought aroma of baking custard tarts and all that is Chinatown.

Quarry

Mist fills the mile-wide Notch between the granite mountains,
　　　massive
Peaks; bald grey and rounded Appalachians
They're touched by cloud-bank, flat, that fills the sky —

At valley-bottoms: villages, their names at first brand-new (to me,
　　　at least)
But then, my memory stirs —

O'Rourke; Franconia; Ellsworth; those the names
We heard those names, long time ago — somewhere —
And suddenly the book falls from the bookcase —

A man splits granite, then he splits the lives of all around him

A wedge forced into notches in the granite
A wedge forced into notches in the egos of contemporaries —
Granite; you can wear it down; but split it and it shatters

And many mallet-strokes are made; your hands are calloused now
Calloused is your mind, as well, but faithfulness, conviction drive
　　　you on

And then, one day, applause — or so you hope —
And meanwhile you will swing that mallet, write these words, and
　　　watch that mist
That mist that fills the mile-wide Notch between the granite
　　　mountains, massive.

Cathy Dreyer

Sappho's Creature and Whizz Hair Remover

After Porky's Hare Hunt — *Leon Schlesinger Studios, 1938*

She does it to Herself / before the war, She
drinks the chemical depilatory / while the pixelated hunter holds
his unpixelated chin / gun forgotten
pointing at the undrawn sky / (these are such early days
childhood / still a wrinkle
in the indices / of notyetwritten books
Bugs Bunny undetermined / *Porky's* work in progress
and, we happy rabbits / without a memory
of genocide / to forget)
the hunter is perplexed / as She depilates herself
as though She were a blemish / a cautionary tale
Our Uncomely Lady / of the Untamed Pits
or a homonym. / Call Her what you like

Look! Look! / She's going … going …

We like to drink with Her
Cos She is wild and free
When we drink with Her
She downs the lot in three! two! one! gone!

The hunter / flailing
in space / the bottle hovers
on gray air / on cartoon
His brain whirling / clutching at
Her not seeing him / a handful of air
like a baby / tries and fails to catch the tit
bewildered by dimension. / Where *IS* She?
Here I am / *Hey! Fatboy!*
She says, / pulling Herself out of Her hat
just out of shot / by those old boots and tyres
and broken drainpipes / the hut's dilapidated

<table>
<tr><td>though this is unexplained</td><td>but 'Of course,'</td></tr>
<tr><td>Marxists know,</td><td>(you know)</td></tr>
<tr><td>'that this means war!'</td><td>and Gable, languid, pronounces</td></tr>
<tr><td>though carrots</td><td>'It's simple:</td></tr>
<tr><td>nothing but carrots</td><td>sounds quite like carrots</td></tr>
<tr><td>no matter how high</td><td>you hitch your skirt.</td></tr>
</table>

(Form devised by Ira Lightman)

Our Subsidiary Arrival (without M.E.N)

After W.B. Yeats

Twist twofold caught by our full spiral
Our hawk without hawk-coach;
Stuff falls apart; hubs fail;
Paltry chaos struts about our world,
Our blood-dull drift flows, plus ubiquitously
Our ritual of purity is sub-thalassic;
Our first class lack all ardour, as our worst
Hold avid sway.

Without doubt a shock is local;
Without doubt our Subsidiary Arrival is local.
Our Subsidiary Arrival! Hardly do such words fall out
But a vast copy of our Spirit of this World
Disturbs our sight: a spoil of arid grit
A spook with big cat body plus this skull of a lad,
A look void plus callous as our vital star,
Drags its slow thighs, as all about it
Roll shadows of our furious dust-bowl birds.
Our apophasis drops, but today I grasp
That colossal shifts of oblivious sprawl
Brought us to toxic stupor cast by a shaky cot,
What rough virus, its hour brought high at last,
Sags towards this holy parish for its birth?

This poem appeared on queenmobs.com under a slightly different title

Sappho's Creature and the
Wild Flowers of the Chalk

This begins as far back in the story as glow
leaves on trees in summer and when the girl I
was would wander up and around the meadows'
White Helleborine.

After some time, people began to say that
Pyramidal Orchid more than other girls.
I was most upset. Adolescents are in fact
Scabious tender.

Seven months passed. *Yellow-wort* was an issue.
Not that I was hairy (or huffy), more that
I was *Pasque Flower* as a girl in tissue:
furry, all over.

Now my bed is sunk in the *Dropwort*, on chalk hills
Winter's *Bee Orchid* in the cold of moon light.
Summer leads me back to the sun and cheap thrills –
bucks with *Two Gentians.*

I enjoy *Wild Thyme* for my tea; the pun is
fun, the stems are chewy and sweet on my tongue.
Grazing may be *Rampion*, though: the penis
can't help its *Rock Rose.*

(Stick to *Horse-shoe Vetch* if you must discourage
Purple Milk-Vetch. It has a quelling power.
I have seen it used with a comic flourish,
what a furore!)

Fights are surprisingly diverting for me.
Landing both feet square on a head is good sport.
Sadly, not all bucks are well-bred so I'm choosy,
playing the *Sainfoin.*

Sappho's Creature Makes Her Bed. Lies in It

Sappho's creature finds a new form. She tests the
wind and turns her back to its force, then bends and
scratches out a minimal ditch in which her
bed will be stable.

For the frame, she tucks in her tail and tips back,
lets her hindlegs stretch to the front, then forms her
smaller forelegs into a delicate rack:
this is her pillow.

Folding forward – ditching herself in plain sight –
she reverts to form, just a lump of damp mud,
clod of dark fur, so that the eye is not quite
sure what it just saw.

She reforms in lightlessness. Blackthorn shadows
scrawl their weathered algebra over her fur,
cool her nostrils, tease her with dark tobaccos
fusing through wet grass.

Hunger rousts her, rips at her guts, deforms her
roaming dreams. Still she hesitates, loathe to lose
all the sweet heat carefully stored in her fur,
warmed by her body.

Sitting up, she breathes in the scents, the sour
signature of chemical formulations
nearly drowning notes of the grass in flower
washed in the night's dew.

Hilda Sheehan

"Dandelions are the kinds of the sunshine you walk past, Weed."

You are so wicked. Did your mother lock you in a dark room? Did she bash your brains with the family brush?

Write as if your pen is trying to kill you.

When did you last kill a poet? I froze one to death with my boredom: eyes made frost-lasers I couldn't control. *Sometimes anger can help you survive.*

The electric meter of my heart is empty of fifties. Use a Rizla to stop the beats – smoke the rest.

You are an invincible child – too big for a boy. We all desire our boyhood. My girlhood got me out of home in the comfort of a man's jacket. It's the gas fire effect. We gather about it from the cold of our beds. The cold of a boy is not equal to the cold of a girl.

Lunch was served with a silk daffodil. I wrote 'SIK' daffodil – dyslexia turns paper yellow – sugar in a 1970s glass-silver fountain.

Can you taste sugar when you write? If not, sit in the sugar a while. Then tip out, tip out.

You have broken my teeth on the goodness of a vinegar bottle est(1794)since. You taste of junk. I am the smell you wish you was.

She who kills laughing is a potted angel. Don't laugh at angels in pots. Angels need freedom to be –

poem = magic life

Addict of cool. Stupid fools. I'll give out dandelions at your funerools.

A man walks into a bar

carrying a baby. A baby, in a bar? Yes. A man walks into a bar wearing nothing but a baby. A baby? Yes. A man walks into a bar singing a baby and the baby tries to sing with him but no one can hear the baby. A man walks into a bar like a baby and the bar man refuses to serve him a drink until he walks properly. Act normal if you want a drink. A man walks into a bar as small as a baby and no one notices him. It's depressing how small he is, it's a sad episode. A baby walks into a bar as big as a man but we all know he's a baby. We put him in a pushchair. The pushchair is placed outside the bar until the man finishes his drink. However, when we go to retrieve the baby the baby is empty and the pushchair is loaded up with sixteen men. Sixteen men in one pushchair? Yes, all the size of babies.

The unpublishable ugly duckling left-overs of the argument for the avant-garde

Imagine me a pen to write this down? Impossible!

What the avant-garde is not: a supermarket for all of poetry to fill its baskets of word product – 15 poets sold 15 poems in as many days = superheroes. It's not a dry-cleaners, or a bookies. The avant-garde is not very poetry trending right now on Twitter. If it's avant-garde, we may not know it yet.

I ask the avant-garde to name names – it says, wait for the 2021 Census to see who is left off the list in the normal houses (servants, whores, bin men) the visitors who birthed poems out of wedlock. Never sell your bastards.

"Which is more avant-garde --- a giraffe or an elephant?" Kenneth Koch. He admired the French surrealists and William Carlos Williams. So many men hiding weird women under Exquisite Corpses. Keep all those women in a precious freedom pin along with Mallarmé. Koch made up a few extra poets to enjoy. If there are poets missing in your life, translate them. Remember the bravery of Cahun on Jersey photographing her resistance of dummies, pocket-filling protest into German soldiers – read her poems and risk your life, get arrested, be naked where naked hurts most. Be sentenced to death.

Why is the avant-garde so short? Probably because it ends so abruptly such as Mew, Wickham or Rimbaud, or the falling old ladies of starved, imprisoned Daniil Kharms: "Well, to Hell with him. Instead, let me tell about Anna Ignatievna. But it is not so easy to tell about Anna Ignatievna. Firstly, I know almost nothing about her, and secondly, I have just fallen off my chair."

There's no harm in deception, the avant-garde comes alive like in the film of Pinocchio. O those poems made of wood telling lies used by the power hungry to string us up for a show. No mention of a wooden boy.

Be kind. Be uncool. Don't give a damn what any magazine or institution thinks. Write without consideration or conformity – confuse your poetry neighbours who say, "carrots would never say that, or do that." – Pedant! Carrots do whatever they like! Remember, your grammar is on the back of a tractor spelt like Mina Loy (that's not her real name). Your career is over in a hairstyle.

Be as intellectual as the self-checkout (which is also avant-garde because technically you can get away without paying) – take no receipts – reject all payments for the stupid books you locked your poems in. Punish every poem in a shrink-wrap stanza – lie them on the floor like a spoilt child: scream them, rise them to the sound of naked lights illuminating her final words 100 years ago, and still as missing:

"She was right to be bright. Edith was right. Scenery is a valley in moon-light." Gertrude Stein.

*Note: This poem came as a result from questions by Caleb Parkin for his recent Poetry School Class, 'Letting Your Avant Garde Down'.

A table is a horse not running

Legs unfinished and those legs are my mothers. A table long, a table full of her regret and plates of guilt. The horse is tied now to the radiator, the radiator is on high, the horse boils over. There's a terrible smell – that of an over-cooked table. We look in shock. What! This table once a horse? Don't say that. Don't think that. Certainly, never eat on such a thing.

The poem shows me a picture of myself

Here, suspended with little nothing on, tied up in various impossible places. Head now unheard of, tied to a chimney of Jackdaws fighting off signals of 'help,' declaring to God. 'No God, No God', they preach. They bring newspaper cuttings, THIS IS THE PRESIDENT or ATROCITY … what are they saying? Head in a jacket to escape the truth. Arms hammered to the pear tree. Do not stop to think of the century. You cannot wave down hope. Where legs swing is a line of nonsense – a bottom is part of a desert and can't reach land – no sea – no forest.

Poem with man in it

I took the poem I'd written you in to the doctors and he confirmed I was very sick, to take it to the nearest emergency room and have it scraped for unpleasant desires, nasty thoughts, adultery. There were no editors on duty but an on-call God offered to drill the magic out of every line. 'Or, you can leave it, see how long it lives without him,' he said.

Jill Jones

this makebelieve this driftwood

this abundance this consumptive force begging the future
this driftwood breaking apart arguments harmonies limbo
this window this plastic viscera amps in the shadows

composing this makebelieve in paragraphs memorising privilege
sand the car sales yard this homecoming orchestra staggering in
cupboards this record jacket dirty open-weave curtains

this background signal phantom washes a broken cup
black with insects knowing this nakedness this chameleon self
spray painting manifestoes 'all doors lead to busy rooms'

gathering happy blues hyperventilating eternal focus restructuring
open-ness bottles of Johnny Walker towers of toilet paper
this cardboard the dog next-door looking through salvage

this flavouring grottoes of biscuits the sound of breaking glass
this earthen darkness anticipating rituals the back room
ask for French 'it's getting too hard' 'no' and 'yes' this mask

brown haze sweeping backwards weather memorising dust
wine and smorgasbord piano accordion classics this stuff
into thousands of pillows pulling apart in shapes of animals

The Scatter Singing

River you step in   a road
Direction litters
in different ways outside   my head

Thank you air, why
I'm here
Thanks dust   all you burials, roads
rocks, the sea   recumbent obstacles

Relax!
Lasting moments   are only moments
        in gardens, on nature strips
I never learned to ride a bike

The colours of things   always change
universal   like the galaxy
You can see some of it
from here on a clear night

Or birds resting in wetlands
How long have they been here?
I don't know   hiding so much

You little dinosaurs of flight
You ancient soundings
And you rightly scatter from me

        Yet, singing

Transcendental Etude

I could never kick the ball hard enough.
The smell of winter is miles off blue.
The world is the handbag, the case, the shit storm.
It's easy to lose sight of the packaging.

I split the celery like an entertainment machine.
The evening moves everything apart.
I dissent again but no-one hears.
I divide time into useful components.

I've been taking the sky literally.
It reminds me of something.
Up there on the wire, in the green clouds.
Although there's nothing transcendental in reach.

Outside there's a pile of yellow petals.
The gates are humming, birds cracking seeds.
I'm cuter than cactus now.
It's better than being slavish.

Everything today is inside itself.
There are too many symbols.
And hell has no high-minded future.
It's not a philosophical argument.

Sun is better this morning.
There should be more butterflies.
From that high up everything shines.
Even the coins we lost.

You walk better than me.
My heartache's softer.
You can hear it dripping.
It's not all fair sailing.

Was it this hot when we were children?
Even angels aren't the same.
They make us restless up there, in the green clouds.
The feathers are moving apart.

Cleave, Carry, Fly

I would be agitated if I had to fly
trying to catch a flower
In the cradle, was I flying?

Sometimes the sky is bronze
Sometimes I can't handle blue

'I am surprised by my own emotional reaction'
The way I cleave to the seat
that 'politics on the outside'

I want to believe I can carry on
'It's just too much work'

I'll sit here. See there!
The magpie cleans its beak
on those curved branches

If I could shun my own lifestyle as
as a model train wrecks itself

'I am surprised by…'
       the way the news
          removes
'…my own emotional reaction'

Fun vaporises

The sky's now almost white
on the northern horizon

There's singing up high

A Foretelling

'everything we say is taped unless we pull the plug'
history's always happening   there's nothing but now
'let's go back to an earlier version'
there's a bird in the tunnel   dying   doing the foretelling
you patch up the vocal   you give it a name
one more time with feeling   'it sounds awesome'
'but the fader does fuck all'   press the buttons anyway
where accidents happen   in the shifty space of jamming
chords are circular   my voice=lost things=last things
invisible things so tiny and huge   the diminishing
my struggle with wires and mind fuck   the modifications
like loose change in your pocket

'is my hair alright'   can I proceed with confidence
is there any point to being kind when air is irritable
when things in the room begin to flicker
when there's nothing left to reheat   avenues collapse
laboratories emptied   they stop giving out water
'would you like it if I told you, if I told you'
you're stretched in another atmosphere
a stringed instrument sidling through time
something shudders behind the horizon   a melody
a malady   a sick flower   whitened death   stuck culture
mould on a field   as government by thievery would let it
all go into their sing-song pockets

'here they come!'   powers!   the old powers looking for a home
approaching   radiating   stars that die for us   the serpents
nests   the fruit   flesh   coats   socks   valves   wheels
the see-through world   the sex of clouds   tyrant mirrors
hooks displacements thread in the machine   another artist
following moments   memory machines   hoping to get lucky
with a chunk of rusty light but the prophets were wrong

it all matters   states of matter   cracked concrete   oil
and breath   your card's no longer accepted at the checkout
a shaky crossing   leaves scratching over the playground
the dead in the parklands   there's no rehearsal
check your pockets!

Come Together

Could we get it together in darkness or reading
by a lamp, living off the grid?
You can see how much brighter it is,
that distribution is more than leaves falling.
Is it a charity deal?

Self-sufficiency doesn't apply to trees.
What is sufficient? Plug and play, the expandable?
If you don't have light, let's get the hang
of these strings. Let's stay in tune.
Vibrato can be an obsession.

Form, function, yay! Test the system.
There's something about tonal quality.
Oh savage breast! Oh valleys of tremolo!
Time is the bigger risk. Be clean and green
or get home early.

Perhaps you'll pick the difference
in dodgy budget figures. Sacked for treason?
That's probably where it went wrong.
Hang onto your brand equity.
Is there worse to come?

Hey big spender, where is everyone gone?
Into the west, into the geek zone
the talent of the sexy beast. In the heart
of the eruption
black light falls on wings.

Drew Milne

In The Forest of Symbols. On the reserve, both formally and informally, any behaviour not given over to technical production was under pressure to owe something to mystical beings or symbols. The legal institution of the forest spoke of Norman deer farms and protein management for aristocrats. This legal fiction secured the domain of stray deer, who could range far beyond wooded lands at the heart of the forest without becoming free game. Although a forest is mostly pasture rather than woods, the physical forest became synonymous with woodland. Deer parks were exported to the highlands, where the symbol became an allegory of human clearances and mere sport. Closer to cities, the sign was given shelter in forests of the night where tigers might dart and fox. The rain forest beckons and the acids sing of tanks. Around the forest of Chernobyl, the ruins of Soviet nuclear power range far beyond the carved up regions that emerged around the agony and the ecstasy of the sarcophagus. Radioactive dust killed off so many pine trees in the red forest, once among the world's most radioactive scraps of land, now bulldozed and buried. Imagine a forest. A real forest. Then flatten it under a cloud of fallout and mulch into a compost under foot. The soil still emits. The lost forest has become synonymous with the physical zone of alienation. Humans are not free to roam around this fiction. Formal and informal relocation conventions pass for polite society, even to the extent of attracting tourists. At the centre of the ancient woods and marshes stood the Partisan's Tree, now marked by a memorial. The borders are based on soil deposits of radioactive materials. At least one church inside the zone claims miraculously low radiation levels. The perimeter is patrolled by horses. Allegories of sustainable growth have nevertheless been glimpsed flitting across pillars of the community. Odours, distress calls and albino mutations form correspondences and are chased down by eco-tourists. The chirrup of geiger counters disturbs the natural rhythms of poachers. But the groves of Chernobyl live in description still, radiating song, harmoniously diffused and well beyond mere legal bounds. The power there laid low sits gloomily over the groves and dispeopled airs. Intimations of cancer trace radiation's fiery scars. The bitter landskip of absent trees grumbles more than it trembles for sylvan strains. Rivers and lakes threaten to spill their silt once the security of the dikes is neglected or overcome by darker weather. Wildfires raise the roof on toxic clouds, while wildlife, loosely framed but externally policed, is left to its own devices. It has been called a nature reserve, but it is also home from home for hundreds of abandoned vehicles, helicopters, ships and barges. The state of the underground military complex is set to become a leading light in the global unconscious.

The virus of the species. The walking shadow took precedence and insisted on italics or deference, or both. Questions about proper nouns often interrupted proceedings but no-one argued for an adjournment. Many diverse viruses saw the sense in coming together under one name. The lack of folk names reflected light recognition of even the most tangible given names otherwise made good by traditional practices. Finders, namers, was the law of the club. The generosity of shared knowledge wanted to draw a line under the difference between a virus and a genus. Proponents of the higher taxonomy behaved like neoliberals, though it was hard to discern liberalism in the ardour for grant capture. An opposing faction sought to overturn the very concept of subfamilies as a derogation of the real. One particularly heated exchange concerned the legacy of horizontal gene transfer. Assuming that the history of struggle was not reduced to evolutionary endgames, the possibility that important transfers went on without going from parent to offspring, punched quite a few holes in the genealogy of life. It was even said that gene transfer shepherded the totality of the biopshere. Genetic engineers were hot for data inflation and grafting. The question of bacterial evolution, before and after the eutherian interlude, turned everything on its head. The biological paradigm is going critical. When a virus was shown to transduce between bacteria, the stage was set for biopolitical war, attended by claims about just wars and medical benefits. The data outgrew the possibility of ethical transfers. Boundaries between species began to resemble artificial lines drawn on a map of human convenience, a mere t-square across deserts of divided ecology. A virus called sputnik was taken as evidence of viral cannibalism. Flailing around for analogies, transfers were assumed to be scaled down versions of human games. Chloroplast and mitochondrial genomes had made the knight's move into the nuclear genome. Malaria was said to have stolen bits of genetic material to convert its human presence from short stay to long stay. There was growing evidence that genetic engineering copied gene transfer through the use of synthetic expression cassettes. Mix tapes were going viral. The metaphor of life as tree became old news as phylogenetic networks came to resemble slime molds. Gene sharing pointed the way to recognition of ancient bonds, and the sharing of the expertise associated with viral nerve tracking. The word parasite had a bitter sweet taste. Attempts to divide up the whole story into bad guys and good took no account of the communality of acquired immunities and microbial persistence. Law become lore overnight. The nerve cells of the most recent research networks promised to keep in touch. There was talk of bringing experts in neuroscience and ancient viruses together to work out the fundamental poetics of zeugma. Grammar was likely to be in for a tough time once debate swung round to the universality of the conjunction. Exchanges between nouns and verbs were heated.

Executive Summary. Plummeting fish stocks undermine existing quotas. Stocks of words still capable of ringing alarm bells are heavily depleted. Soundbite quality has fallen victim to disaster fatigue. Amid dwindling confidence in what once appeared to be natural abundance, the widespread destruction of lexical habitats endangers even the very signs of alarm that called for renewed discard bans. The turd in the bath is aquaculture, sometime oxymoron that gave rise to the concept of wild fish. Fish farms are a stain on lyric ponds. The build-up of mercury makes for gut-wrenching reading. Farmed salmon are doused with hydrogen peroxide to kill off sea lice, but resistances gather. The trends are nevertheless rocketing to record lows, with unprecedented levels and shocked scientists. The naturalist novel becomes a fairy story. Repetition implies familiar conclusions,

conclusions that might preserve something out of precipitous collapse. But fish feel pain. Their gods are unsung. The nine daughters of Ægir personify wave characteristics, though the pelagic gods pushing back against ocean-going trawlers are notable by their absence. Stocks of caught fish are said to be gravitating towards affluence, as the dead migrate from the more to the less needy. Today's fish are tomorrow's fossils. The fishprint of globalisation extends beyond the oxymoron of territorial waters. The coelacanth, celebrated Lazarus of human taxonomy, gives hope that the electrosensory world of fossils might not be extinct. A spokesperson for fish declared that they wanted their waters back.

Khaled Hakim

Ben Hur

Dear B

Do you remember wen I ran to Stockwel or Brixton tube to catch y/ bifore yoo disapeared to say I do love yoo.

Perhaps yr superier brittelnes & my superier horsshit wil alwayz get in th way. Evrything is fin if we tawk abot the England cricket teme.

I dont kno if im riting this 2000 yers ago – I wish y/ cd forget.

But I did catch yu up & y/ understood

our diferent tradicions hypostasized as Poesy: the rize of the middle-clases & hysteria.

Did I tell yu th storie I told Reds & owr cuzins. Y/ kno how they wd mythologize my brekfast – no actuelly I wud mythologiz it for em.

I, Judah Ben Hur colecting comunity memory as isolated bed sors.

This WPC tekkin my statement wile the paramedicks ar sticking him on a stretcher & shes woried im spasd out. Id probably shoplifted somthing.

I was in this Camden charity shop & theze 2 goyim are having a set-to on th steeming Hiy St, & the sqwat ponytail goy daring this shwartz, lyk – *Make yer moove – Com on then...* I thawt th Nubian bloke was interfering with his car.

The ponytail coms in, all chuffd & ses *Hes a pervert.* I says Wot. He seys – *hes using a mirrer to look up wimens dresses.* Ten minits later th schwarz coms in & hes saying *So ya think yer hard yeah*, & hez holding this brown paper bag handle thing wich I think is th ladys miror, the empiricist metafors alibi. & i gos behind him to I dunno, get in if it starts.

Al hell braks loose the glass lamps & ornaments, its raining shards the Nubians thrusting *thuk thup* & ponytails throwing punches & they get in this clinch. I jump on his back & hawl him off & i dont kno he must hav sqwirm out; the goy whos stabd lungez over me & falls over all th shatterd bric a brak theyr chucking pots & vazes at eche other.

Im folowing th Mamluk on Camden Hiyh St, i seys to th Ponytail whos coming back, *Yoo stabbd,* & i see him holding th plase. I folow the Mamluk thinking Im Famus Five. Anyway he givs th slip on Greenland St Schmeenland St. Ive bin heer befor, the yuneeq event wich maks meening thru history, thru, becus.

Is that my lot — som banal urban awthenitissity? Im not mekin another racist racionale soothsay.

A poem crys denial. O displasd comunitarians. O jihadless jobless. From lyf without Royal Colege of Art to the life of twiliyht press within. Waz, is ther, shal it. Egh?

(But our cuzins loved th story. Did I tell yu how I tole peple in Bangladesh a slihte scar on my cheek was from a nife fite. I think it was a bad shaving insident. But I beleved it myself. Fufoo was saying I shud sort owt prayr duties as the prospectiv child brides a strickly pius family)

I, Judah Ben-Hur went strait to th denotativ wich sed *I am pleazd* or *I am sorry.* & thers a feeling I slipt down a pasage of posible dimensions; ther wus the other spasetyme i opend th letter & clench a fist. Ther was a posibility the letters alter as aberacion of mind. The racionalist cognitiv senterd explanasions dont hold water when yore th Hero

mihty passions at boiling point & loud theatrickal tunes; think we missd th bote.

Brodcast engineers track narativs scope, rerite the descriptiv moovment disclozing the Word the fatherless myth, reproducing anti Roman paradise. Fiht an idea with another idea! The ideology smashing superstructurs of plural poetriz!

Were ther is grate power, graet empire, grate feeling – error creeps in

the stone that fel from this room is still falling

not tears for the parents deth, but tears for speeches prohibicion; O lineal imperativ! O wifely unknown!

all acros the empire peple fite complecions family, clozurs marrige. Only I rite pulchritudes deceet. O line of softnes & conceet.

It goz on – it goes on Judah – th race – is not – over...

but lov them in the way they need to be lovd, as if yoo had never been heer

...

Deer B, I only had the haziest recolecksion of his fase. I tell ya wen i wen in to do the ID parade with the others, they cald me & my hart starts thumping liyk *I* wus gilty.

Luckily the goy with the ponytail told me hed trawld round in a polise car after he got owtta hospital & pointed him out at Camden Tube. So al I had to do waz pick owt the won closest to th story.

Th Kush barstard kept geting th trial put off for months. But when it got ther he was pleeding provocasion. He got 5 yers. His defendant got on me how exacly it started cauz wat I remember he started trashing th lamps befor he went for him, but I musta got it rong, whaddo I no –

We are th lost benefit seekers, we are all rowing a slavship to Lidl – hoo knew 4000 *shahids* are stacking shopping trolleys wayting for a conflagracion of th hart.

My empiricist metafor is catching a traine to Birmingum – running to say *I do lov yoo*.

If Ben Hur can tuche his sister the leper…

Here is a coache of feeling. Therr is a coche of sadnes.

I dremed I cawt yoo in a bistro & i was in my dresing gown – its still 2000 yrs ago but set in the prezent.

Ther is retirment doggerel. A green spinster gable. A sadnes room.

Ilford 1998 / London 2018

Barbara Tomash

from Her Scant State

Trouble was the condition she fully measured at the window leaning far out. (To say something really human, I discovered ugliness.) An anticlimax. She was trying to see child, childbirth, little girl, home from nurse, never a word, my dear_____. On her lips an echo. Exhausted. She had lost the conditions, the little girl, his wife, the question, the troubling pledge, the brief happiness. That had cost her. The real mother had shed any abundance. Yes, sufficiently.

*

Her voice strange and her eyes widely open, daughter—very quiet, very convenient, most liberal—as if looking at the basket of flowers. Putting a thing into word pictures an essential need in families. This little sketch. Delicate organism of daughter. To mark the difference between careful finishing touches. A chill. A home. The old Protestant tradition. And so many pretty banishments.

Her compassion concealed history, as I believe you like it. Exquisite, impressive, sad. Don't try to frighten me. Because you fatigue yourself, I've given you an interest in detachment. Certainly it helps. This winter brilliancy unable to be bewildered. I've a great need to suffer alteration. To start with the way we're to end. Coldness, how we're to end. Common crimes giving an extreme effect to her hand quickly. Beautiful. Anyone's valuation of anything. I have made her that?

★

Her money. Sleeping. Burned the pretty word roots in the open air. Rake the soil. The circle round which she walked. In strange exercises. She held her bouquet. "I'm afraid you wouldn't give it back."

★

Little black dress, gently stroked hair, the room arranged well—no right to criticize. Husbands and wives as magnificent as two saints, their painted heads an awful phenomenon. "You must never say that." With her hand on the latch—kissed her. Kissed the dusty, smoky years before. Can I stop with her?

Note: These pieces are excerpted from an erasure of Henry James' novel *The Portrait of a Lady*.

Janet Sutherland

You hold in your head a notion of the land

You squatted, shat and wiped your bum
with dock leaves. You trotted in amongst
the giant cows. Off you went in shorts,

bare chested, or in woollen balaclava,
stirrup pants and anorak. You didn't care,
you were in woods, inventing houses

with your sister, out of baler-twine and twigs,
and though you were a few yards off the path,
you were in wilderness, alive and lost.

★

At twelve you learned to drive the little Fergie,
your father taught you how to start it up
and demonstrated how to stop. He let you

work out how to steer. You aimed between
the gateposts at the end of *Muddy Track*
and felt the steering wheel go racketing about,

the tyres run slantwise over stones.
You made it through the gateway into *Park*
and pushed the throttle lever up to full.

★

You walked in storms so violent the cows
could not be turned to bring them in.
They stood, backs to the wind, implacable.

You know the rain in horizontal rods,
the drifted snow that lingered for six weeks,
the layered fog they anchored in like boats.

You've felt the sun that dried up everything,
burning all summer till the fields were brown;
the fields that greened-up four days after rain.

★

You've found the afterbirths still lying
in the field like pallid liver strung with rags,
chased with the rainbow oil-slicks of decay

on blood-streaked grass and trampled undersoil.
You've seen calves born, shut them in pens,
and heard their mothers' bellowing.

You set that grief aside. You taught
calves how to dip unwilling heads to drink,
to suck your milky fingers like a straw.

★

In June the sisal strings made welts across
your palms from hay bales packed too tight
or damper than they should have been.

You begged a trailer ride from *Stony Ground*,
five layers up on top of all the bales. You saw
two bales shake loose and burst on stubble.

You yelled for him to stop, he didn't hear.
You rode the earthquake, laughing like a lord,
clinging on but loosened from the world.

★

On summer evenings after school you stacked
the haybarn to its rafters. You stood above
your father while the escalator grabbed

each bale with metal tines and clanked it up.
You tied the rows in, just like bricks,
until you'd raised them to the rooftop furnace.

A cell made hotter and more cramped
by each new bale you pummelled into place.
His tallest ladder sprung you out of jail.

*

You hold in your head the seasons fruitful
and the seasons on a knife edge.
You'd hear the worried voices after school,

Why had Mabel died of bloat? Then watch
him phone the knacker for next morning.
The knacker's van with flatbed, chains

and winch would haul her in and take
her off the field. Her body useless now,
no milk, meat, money, and no breath.

*

You've seen your mother fall and fall,
and fall and fall, never cry, though you've
heard her slur,

you've heard her sentences disintegrate
and you've interpreted. You'd like to hear
her voice again, its undertow has faded.

You'd like to milk the cows with her and wash
their filthy udders with a cloth. You'd like
to tell her what you should have said before.

To the Nightjar

i.m. Margaret Godell, Southwold c. 1548

Her William in his will:
Item, I will have a priest to Rome
to sing for me the space
of one whole year
and I will that the said priest
have for his labour fourteen pounds

★

in a gorse grey common
a handkerchief held up
will call the nightjar to his song

★

a rising clatter-churr, a soft *coohwick*,
uneven wing claps, like an audience of one
unsettled by a play as the curtain falls

★

corpse fowl, puckeridge, flying-toad,
fern-owl, night-hawk, moth-owl,
dorhawk, churn-owl, eve-jar, wheel-bird,
gnat hawk, night swallow, nightjar,
nightjar, nightjar

★

Item, I give to my said wife
one of my two ships
the Cecilly or the Andrew
and I will that Margaret, my wife
shall have my place called Skylmans
with all the lands, tenements, rents and services…

upon condition that the said Margaret
shall find a secular priest
to sing in the church of Southwold,
during her life aforesaid,
for my soul

*

In the broad space between
day and night and
out of the half-seen woods
who sings for the soul of Margaret Godell?
I, said the Nightjar, *with my jarring rattles, wing-claps*
I sing for Margaret
an unpaid plainsong
for her room in heaven.

for the blacksmith who painted himself as a boy

as a boy at a ford, as a boy larking about with his friends at a ford, with his friends leaping into the river, as a boy in a river, as a loose-limbed beautiful boy, as a boy fractioned, as zinc-white water weeping from his limbs, as a river, as a bank where all the trees are brown, where earth is brown, and brown leaves hang in unlit trails to the brown water, as a river, as a strong river carrying the bodies of boys above and within itself, as a brown light on broken water, as a room with a brown river in it, as a pool, as a likeness of a river, as a man dreaming, as an angularity, a frame, a pattern roughed out with callipers, a ration, a toll, a clang or a peal, as a resemblance, as no resemblance, as a tempering for taps, dies, drill bits, hammers, cold chisels, as a quench, as a man drowning, as a knock or a strike, as water is, as a plain river, as a loose-limbed boy.

Everyday Ataxia

for Paddy

A fly specked bulb might rock her from her feet
as she lurches home from the milking parlour
distempered brick will prop her if she stumbles
and brush the cotton of her milking coat with chalk.
The drip at the end of her nose says it's winter
and calves make little murmurs as they settle.
I know this route, the sugar beet in bins
dried to its shredded twists, the swathes of filthy cobwebs
pocketing the window,
the floor drifted with barley straw, spilled Denkavit
and all along the corridor she's held
by places to lean, places to grab a hold
until she sets her sail to tack the fifty yards towards the house –
black grass, cold stars, a rolling ocean.

At Cuckmere

Down in the ditches reeds eat mud and on the hills
cows turn to sniff at their calves as if they were
strangers. This river's a snake that opens its mouth
and sings, looping and undulating, leaving
a sloughed skin oxbow wrinkled by its side,
but neither ditch nor oxbow will take us back home.
The real snake in the old river does that,
swimming head up and jaunty across a ford,
through muscled water, cold and treacherous,
where we still paddle; our luminous shins
skinny, white as the peeled sticks we use
as switches. "Christ!" he says, "look at that
snake swimming". Heifers stand in the shallows,
snorting and shaking off the flies before they drink.

Martin Corless-Smith

Samson Beleaguered (his blindness/death)

If I tried to recall
The specifics of a scene
One place, as the impulse
Of writing truthfully
What would that mean or matter
In this world?

The bars of the winter heater
throw their orange glow
onto our faces in the frigid gloom
With the bedroom window ice
outlooking the pale sky above
scrappy nests of neighbour fencing

A blue glass angel bear
Barely an inch high
From the chemist's door
Appears in my hand and

I will be lifted by love
And the cold gloved mother
Into a yellow flower
As if my eyes were water jugs
with a gentle breeze upon

A diet of feathers and
A diet of flies
As my bare parts
Hang through the wire grate

Always and often again recall
Her kindness towards

Me above all
And the pleasure I held
In forgetting that.

Taking his life
In an avenue of limes
with the cool water left
half-finished by the chair
as blossom and snow wheels through the air.
Enough of the building remained to appear
Once grand
With the do not enter
Sign on the door
Put down the shopping
Too heavy to bear

Wreck of the Sisterland

Boats boast across the skein
Skinny mast a cross masters
The wind sheets of rain
Skin the winding sheet remains

When in lust we drown
Downed a lashing—weather
The leather hide—wet inside
Her lengthening—lists to one side

She male replaces the dream
She'd made—a moon's face
Then the sun's reflection upon
Deemed too close to the room's embrace

I can't recall in darkness
The damp rat barks in the hall
Red-eyed cunt—the dank carpet
Car headlights—rolled up wet joint.

Sister on her haunches over the pit-
style shitter after bad peaches
Her hairy golden paunch and bear tattoo
I see her drain her spew & shit

Permanent loss—the beach recedes
Past the post of private property
Sperm enters the host—reaches
The ocean held for public use

Her pubis—the untying of a gown
After sickness and the tidying self groom
With warm flannel—rich green cotton
Turns brown—ready to reach again.

Stiff-pricked afternoon—a study
Shuttered from the day—barely a view
Sliver of thigh white against van dyke brown
Palming the rose tip stuttered into use.

★

The thrown-up raging blue
A cup of agency sky crack
Seated on a throne—aging child
Between trees—bright green leaves—ascend.

Tea thru tea—fuck you china
I go for Darjeeling—read the leaves—lucky
That I'm on a journey—then later
After tea the quick descent—the laughter.

Coleridge's mirror

this small desert-like
winter in England
a disaster with soot
old as the houses
cut in half
the mirror wall
the exhausting terror
of falling over.

Scythe like lemons
On bitumen field
Lamp light & helios
Three feet above

A moth fell Andromeda
Oh my only
Ask
When I was young enough
To fit under the table
& lick the leg.

Reading on the afternoon bed
Let my feet get cold
A square of yellow—a triangle of green
Then mauve then death our truest friend.

William Langland dreams of the new millennium

On naugahyde recline, the daffy muse
Is insolent—no emails for a week
I can only hope that what I spent a lifetime mustering
As knowledge or forgetfulness will visit when I speak—
Use all the totems of my failed conjuring
I calm the desert, dust the Malvern Hills
And sleep with many jobs undone—
Small minnows in a sombre shake
Anon the move these niggles in a shoal
To bury any impetus—all fellow men are now indifferent.
All. Shakespeare on Shaftesbury Avenue. Milton in the Peaks.
The squalid occupancy of high offices has revealed the cull.
Wend with irregular beat and mount a post card
On the mantelpiece for your defence—Drum with the marching hosts
From late breakfast of toast and marmalade to roasting meats,
Where after constitutionals are facts or hopes?
A solemn council held in Pandemonium
With powerpoint and overheads and handouts handed out,
Forlorn practise has absolved the schools of any thoughts—
Shout at the end of Parliament, the term is dulled & run,
Routed by a cancer of its self-involvement, like
The human caterpillar marched onto the Vaudevillian Pariah
Of national news. And natural laws such as the
Waves of energy that makes the object thus appear
Has suffered interference—smiling child—each generation will
Supply a chance occurrence of a modicum of mediocre will.

Carrie Etter

Dirge

from *Grief's Alphabet*

Amen and behold, Bernadine,
cantankerous, capacious calls down
down echoing echoing fertile fields
growing garrulous here   here   here
into (justice) jeweled jams, jellies,
(justice) juices knocking, keeling....

Light makes new our project, our plea:
remember, revive. Soon the tillage,
the undulating vacancy, its xenial yield
zones a bounty. (*Bernadine....*)

This Kind

slow now the liquefaction of an August walk

naught but sun overhead, no trees' canopies broad enough to

& humid: ah Illinois, your give & take, give & take

every animal has found shade: cat on porch, dog under tree

only I take the cement line and sense steam rising

remember my father's story: a heat wave in Saint Louie,

eggs fried on the sidewalk

The Many

And now the unbridling: I cut the straw circling the stems, and whoosh! the blooms, the scarlet, the white, the green (two bodies wrestling together, mouths, hands, limbs aflurry....), *this, here, now* of colour (of taste, of touch), of the nipped bouquet resuming the meadow – and yet not (O the morning). The marble floor of not. The stone wall of *who did you think you*. Once the flowers have been scissored from their roots, what did you – I see a young woman, just down the terrace, who from taut uncurls and rises and collapses and I can't say, can I, how many she is....

Trumpicana
A found poem

Check out the new Tropicana website with information on the delicious Tropicana range, new recipes and find out the benefits of 100% pure fruit juice. 'What separates the winners from the losers is how a person reacts to each new twist of fate.' – Donald J. Trump *Tropicana Twist Skirted Swimsuit: Complete with a plunging neckline, vibrant tropical print and loose skirted fit, you'll love how confident this colourful swimsuit makes you feel.* Trump admits to 'feeling up' Melania in public in newly released tapes. *An injured person is tended to in the intersection of Tropicana Ave. and Las Vegas Boulevard after a mass shooting at a country music festival.* During a 2016 Republican debate, the real estate mogul said he carries a gun in his home state of New York, 'sometimes a lot.' *Tropicana Realty is your boutique real estate and property management firm. We are focused on offering exceptional service to our clients in Central Texas.* Trump in Texas: 'I'm the builder president. Remember that.' *Tropicana Homes is the largest and most trusted homebuilder in El Paso.* In 2010, a 131-mile fence was built separating El Paso, Texas and Juárez, Mexico. *Just east of El Paso, Horizon Hills offers convenience, recreational areas, and a rural hush.*

All the tropicanas, the long tremulous, the Trump-thrown hush....

Dirge

from *Grief's Alphabet*

alack bereft be be be carcass
castaway down end, far gone,
heft illustrative just knack.
Lo, my naïve, nest of possibilities
quietly run south to the upswell,
verging woe, (e)xamination, zephyr: alack.

Robert Sheppard

from It's Nothing

(Variation on) Ode to Life

I share a fish's unblinking view of rain on a river surface
under Lime Street station roof glass in the storm. Half
empty mid-afternoon train slips out into weather,
my mind half made up, half blowing free as though

on the platform at Edge Hill. David Bowie's dead;
yet posing by The Wall he's defiantly alive.
Floods mirror watery sun fringed by pressing cloud.
Inside: warmth, coffee. Decision making as poesis…

The train slides under the latticed crystal of Crewe
for pause. In the rhythm of yes and no, between
work and poetry, inside and outside motion and stillness

Don Pullen coaxes, knuckle-slaps, hammers his *Ode to Life*
to life; all I want is to word its wordless asperities into
this poem that will never stop

'Useless Landscape'

This song weighs the same in Tom Jobim's mouth
though its title floats free in mis-transliteration.
It takes on Wittgensteinian mass but
depresses the grace and gravity of *Without you*

it's nothing. On Church St, one of Loy's mad bums
grunts into the plastic *Intonarumori* of a toy
mic and guitar, nothing-words. Modern
boys with virginal giggles fix him

in a phone's stare, knockabout flailing:
this pitiless marionette, who could have translated
the *sotto voce* patter of wild rain for *her* brute ear...

A sharp shard in suspense meshes the patterns I find:
formal collisions hoisted. Freighted by sandbags,
ballast is sinking; the banners frap free.

> *(amid and between Melissa Gordon's* Fallible Space,
> *for Sandeep Parmar)*

Tamar Yoseloff

Anti-midas

Everything he touches turns to shit:

silver sucked of its glitter, bankrupt;
smooth skin shrivelled, breasts sapped.

He balls his fists in his pockets,
but his eyes spread manure in the flowers,

his stare sinks joy, his cesspit heart
seeks the charred core of the sun.

He tries to run, but his feet have slabbed
to stone, he is halted in the mire

of hatred. This is the world he's made,
although he's quick to pass the mantle

to the next man – his curse, his disease.
He breeds dirt from dirt,

his cry is a wheeze in the dark:
Help me. Dig me out.

Occupation Road

We had enough for a couple of weeks, tins of beans, tins of fruit.
We tried to pass the time although all the clocks had stopped. We
shuffled cards, their flat patterns and quaint queens soothing. We
built transistors from scratch but they picked up nothing but hiss.
Everything tasted of tin; I worried it was coming from inside me.
You were certain they'd erect cities on our garbage, write sagas in
a language we'd never live to speak. The train stammered over the
tracks at dusk, cargo scuttling to the far districts.

James Bell

nine sonnets

one stands close by on the edge of the sandbar
a counterpoint to the six who stand in straight arpeggio
much further over
                                a distant music unheard

notation   though cormorants rarely make a sound

this visual can be made in words
there is the temptation to invent
in order to see everything in the round

it is your inclination
                                a parting of the way
that began with cuneiform and now exists
as transparent shadows in a lighted box

two cormorants turn somersaults in the water
each turn under with a set hiatus of thirty seconds

~

from underwater the surface is broken in a quick swallow
for air   cormorants tumble like water acrobats
as a girl sashays past in a dress the wind ripples
against her legs and her mind somewhere else

two boats have shifted sideways on the opposite bank
inclined towards the water with
a perspective not too good to be true for art's sake

these are the leavenings   the semblances
of core reckoning you find where there are senses
of different passages   you breathe air at all times

the river speaks its own language with regular lapses
into a silence where you need to make up the words
place contempt in what would have been said otherwise

decide that silence can always be an opinion

~

language is an acquisition you gain
with practice and repetition
                              the constant sound

waves generated by the wind to a pattern
where there is no code to break and then complete—
silence is never an utterance
                              though nothing is a vacuum

river sounds are joined up   a continuous sigh
of ripples that can build into the storms you dislike

today you sense an evenness though it's too late now

for the cormorant to fly downstream at midday punctuate the chatter
at least help to complete a sentence before going

cormorants could be a new beginning
where the interpretation of what you see is your own

is a spell to conjure in a penumbra
is a sequence that has to be arrived at in time

~

the water is flat and reflective
its shimmer and shimmy has a sensuous appeal

from a distance it looks still while up close
the view you take in is different livelier

the relationship becomes more complex
than a distant ardour or admiration

there are parallels you know of break
down into atomic sizes more infinite

than the one before often viewed
though rarely acknowledged older

akin to love unmet for several years
it either starts again or there is a quick parting

the water is flat and reflective
you see more in it than you did yesterday

~

this morning five cormorants   up close
on a sand spit in the river middle   stand
or swim   take sun with outspread wings

from one angle make black cameo presences
against water reflect silver   their companion
curlew prods deep into the wet sand
as a busy body who pries below their elegance

there is silent water to match usually silent birds
who cull the river for their share of fish
who cannot waste breath with each underwater hunt –
for the moment they stand in surveillance
of the day to come   their shapes represent daily questions

you feel a sharp coolness now each morning
within scenes that imitate peace

~

rain breaks whatever spell there has been
shakes out of shape the kiss of imagination
that stands in the way of reality

54

there is a rush of water downriver
after an all night roar of storm there is a patter
of thoughts as you walk

wonder about the sound
of a voice heard for the first time
in a long time and heard now with a different tone

the music is more sharp   though not a tune
you would dance towards as it beckons

the rain stops
you watch the sun re-emerge while still in shelter
and prepare to continue this journey

~

it takes a long time before you meet the sun
for it makes long shadows even at midday
and disappears into the ground at four

after a cursory journey over visible horizons
it enjoys the tilt to the earth as its vanity

you are content to sit before its radiance and look
at the scene through sunglasses
while the curlew has persistent pecks at wet sand

the boat you call an ark has not gone yet
know there is still time
to gather your thoughts with a few possessions

before the sun goes again you too must move
or be forced to run with the herd
or beg a place aboard the ark to sail at daybreak

~

tide turn is quick   unexpected   quicker
than you would have thought   one way
one second   another second turned round

pushes back towards the sea again
you are the only one who has stopped   nobody
else has noticed the shift in emphasis

you like this yet wonder about the distance
others are from the nature that is them
lives alongside continues
not to dictate a button press existence
a prophet of doom who merely observes
you do not plead stand daily on the border
between the natures of land and water
there is dampness and cold you move on

~

the river is in recovery from a weekend storm
its chill brown water flows down
with gulls on board for the ride

the only constant has been lichen
clung fast to timber quay stanchions

an old man pokes his stick amongst driftwood
stranded on the slipway and drying in the sun –
an accidental wildwood sculpture installation

above the current waterline – part of the cycle
along with cold wind in a low winter sun

you watch the old man leave with nothing –
part of the cycle when others come to look
at this place where its deeper face is unchanged –

you'd like to consider lichen again

Martin Anderson

Road to the North

"Homeward you think we must be sailing
to our own land."
Homer — *The Odyssey* [X: 538–539]

I

Suddenly at the end of day, spectral tree blown
against the window, my father appears before me
marching, leading a shabby contingent of ghosts.
They pause, and then, the sound of half empty
canteens slopping at their waists, approach. I watch them
as if through a stirred-up haze of dust, fragments
from a broken century, their laughter
and song drifting, as they march,
through time's porous and permeable borders
into our own, dissolving all horizons
and distances, shedding the dead weight
of months and years, to appear before
me, reinvigorated. Ghosts, feeding on my blood.

II

I ask him how they managed to arrive, unscathed
out of that gloom at the world's end. "Although
we summoned ourselves" he said "we were loath to
come back, knowing the way, that it would hold for us
only professed guilt. But for pity of you, and to see you
once again and warn you, before the clouds of darkness
block, finally, any hope of return … On the way
by which we came, city after city, nothing but a heap
of smouldering stones, smoke, soot strewn mosques,

hospitals, bodies piled up on pavements, waiting.
As if entire countrysides and cities had been
offered up as burnt sacrifices to the god Mithra,
their odours pleasing to him. An ancient temple to him
preserved, parts of it, in the basement of the House
of Finance which, as we came closer to you,
we saw rising, all steel and glass, like a lance head
flashing under cloud, tilting at the very heavens
themselves. And all around us at night FIRE
the sleepers in untold doorways and hauling,
during day, bags stuffed with their possessions
from bench to low wall to under a bridge
out of the rain. Like those groups of vagabonds
listlessly adrift roaming the turnpikes after their
land was seized, their towns pulled down about
their ears, centuries ago. Home is always the model
for the export of devastation. In fading light we heard
the clank of uncoupled cars in the goods yards and,
from them, a low and muffled tune of despair. Its refrain
rings in our ears, still…"

III

He went on, measuring, carefully, his words: "Conscience,
as we set out, compelled us to re-visit the very places
where we had inflicted so much pain on others; not to
relinquish to forgetfulness, by one ounce, the weight of
our degeneracy. And to show you, in one broad sweep,
both your inheritance and our burden. So we began
where experience first indicted us … Exhausted by heat,
some apoplectic, we dropped like flies by the roadside,
where they buried us. Our cemeteries marched with us,
boon companions, always at our side or behind us,
whispering, laughing. Incised in stone, nameless –
most too low in rank to warrant more than 'private soldier' –
we were left behind; no loved ones who would come
grieving for us later, on that road to the north,
Uttarapath they call it, would be able to find where

we lay. Wormsmeat. Slowly ingested and excreted;
our boots laid with us in that night in case we might
rise up and take again to walking…" And I thought
I caught on the air, for one instant, the smell of
stale sweat and moist leather, of scorching dust.

IV

Noticing the torn and scrofulous uppers
of their boots, I pitied them; that, stirring out of Erebus,
they'd had to traverse its smoke-filled chasms of
vaporous, blood-soaked roads to reach us. "My son" he said
"one need go no further than the nearest manhole and
pry off its lid, to let the fistula's dark stream that's
always under your feet, its rustling skin of vapours,
escape: here; where lies are roared out loud, where
the deepest vein of villainy is silence. The majority,
disdaining the stench, slam back the lid at once.
Few dare to linger over what so deeply offends
their sense of who they are: saviour or slaughterer?
We are not, my son, what we so flatteringly imagine
ourselves to be. But comfort makes cowards of us all.
Let us continue, then, our blighted wanderings
so you may better grasp our burden, your inheritance…"

V

"At night when we lay down under a large white
moon, tongue stuck within moistureless mouth, the
mosquito net shimmered as we moved. Then I imagined
there ran, like a ripple on the air, the sound of the
ice-wallah, his slow methodical jog and 'make-way' cry,
balancing the weight at each end of his pole. Under
the dark dust from burning villages we rested, beside
shutters speckled with it. Yes, our faces still tingling
from the blaze, 'rested'! Night tightened the
throat of thirst. I listened. In his cry, I imagined

59

the desert retreating further and further. And on a road
overgrown with our headstones I dreamed
it was raining: and off a square in Haifa, where
they next posted us, where the letters we kept writing
each week never came back to us unopened, there
were gardens and fountains, and the fragrance of cool
courtyards. But no wounds, no doors of blood needing
scrubbing … But, of course, there would be many such doors
in houses of stone that had stood there countless
generations. And all of them, before they were kicked-in,
daubed as with an invisible blood-marking…"

VI

"At the edge of desert steppe were groves of date palms.
Dates and dung we called it. The camp. D and D. Knee deep
in dates and camel dung. Some rolled their cigarettes from it.
Little did we know what was to come. And in the evenings we fell
about to yarning about our days together on the Grand Trunk
Road. Said we remembered most the smells of spices and
incense intertwined with dust. Not that they weren't present
where we were. But less intense, varied. Remembered the
wayside shrines brightly bedecked, athrong with people. All that
colour, farrago of activity. And then the stillness, and the
silence after, in shadow under the banyan. Adoze at midday,
when the sun was at its highest. Them – not us. Our boots
marching, always marching. And the dhaba, the road-
side eateries. Flatbreads crisping over coals. Every day was
Shrove Tuesday! And onward it went, over fifteen hundred
miles, broad and smiling. Old hands from those parts,
with a smattering of Hindi, waxed lyrical (ah, nostalgia, it is a
dish one never tires of eating) about the coasts,
port-cities where their fathers settled and traded. Where,
bunnias told them, even the parrots once spoke in five languages
when the trade routes were open and flourished. But
where, last century, when our presence became too much
of a burden to them, all that remained was soot blackened

burnt out bungalows and stations. And then gallows.
Lynchings that went on for years. Every 'nigger' (one old hand
mimicked the distress on the bunnia's face) they came
across strung up. Shot. Or bayoneted. Man. Woman. Child …"

VII

"Years later, chest deep in water, waiting
for the small boats to ferry us, ranged out along
the shore, all I could think of was sand
and the abandoned roads which ran off
into it, the villages and towns which we pulled
down without compunction. And those we left
standing, bereft, without a home or food
or means of subsistence, in their own country."
His eyes lowered upon his hands, as if suddenly
they had become the seat of all impurity,
transgression, and stayed there a long time, even
after he resumed talking. "And even later still,
many years on, after we had left that cold, grey
northern coast, re-posted to another, warmer
country, in their eyes whenever they met ours,
in their pained look of scrutiny, I was reminded." Again
he stopped, again looked at his hands. "Of what?"
I asked. "Of fear. In our own. That went
unacknowledged. Of the order, months later,
to burn. Burn all the crates. So many of them.
Crammed with files. And to rake, and re-rake, all
the waste, reduced, already, to ash. And to make
sure nothing of it survived that was not
'broken up'. Fear. Theirs, that gave the order.
And ours. In a crateful of ash. So desperate
to extinguish what, in all those records of
organised violence and inhumanity, proved us inferior
to those we slanderously depicted as inferior
to ourselves. Fear. Of exposure, and of obloquy …"

VIII

Another of the regiment, flaxen haired, still with the
cloud of an untimely death hovering about him, who,
with my father, had survived to reach the beaches
where they stood, waiting to be taken off, but who,
weakened by fatigue and cold, had drowned before
they could haul him aboard, spoke, in a lifting Antrim
accent: "We were, like someone wrote, no more
than 'uniformed assassins'. Nothing we, or our leaders,
did could atone for the misery we'd inflicted earlier
on so many innocent of any crime but trying to live
in their own country ruled by their own kind.
Fleeing, later, through the city where most of us
would eventually embark, I stumbled onto the black
cobblestones, tripped by a fallen wire. All the
telegraph lines were down. Your father helped
me up and I limped off, half walking/trotting
and looking frequently back for any sign of the
pursuer who, at that very moment, was doing no more,
or less, than we had for untold years been doing –
crossing the borders of a sovereign country in force
to take and claim it as our own. And in some cases,
where they wouldn't put up with it, exterminating
them." He shivered. Then shuffled. Tugged his collar
up … "In truth", my father concurred "it could be said
that before we were the victims of those who
pursued us, we were their accomplices, preparing
the ground for the horrors that were to come…"

IX

At first light I saw my father's figure at the window
wavering, its outline against the stirring undulations
of lace, from a breeze out of darkest Erebus,
bending with them, and shedding that semblance
of solidity it had retained for the journey to us.
As I moved towards him his form stabilised. I drew back.

"We'll soon be gone" he said. "Here, fear bred out of greed,
bred out of loss of trust, urged us, dead spirits, back. 'Thieves
and liars' we were called, when living. Justly. For that
our souls scald, simmer. On burning sand. On live coals. Daily.
Nightly." The window rattled to a sudden gust, pushing
the pane in then pulling it back. "Put no faith in good
works. They only paper over cracks. It's here", pointing to
his chest, "work's done. Here alone. Trust no ones word.
But when they act, weigh stated intent with consequence
– to see if they are one. That way you'll drive out the rat
beneath the pile. A lifetime's work. You'll get
little help. Good luck … Here, from what we've seen,
perjury, in all spheres of public life, is not a crime.
So with the law at large, home and abroad. Ignored.
Bent. Or remade. To fit the purposes of the rich, the
powerful … The day they wrenched that flagstaff out of the
lawn in front of Government House, sweating and silently
cursing, they merely thrust and planted it in another
land. Later, in another form. Right through the heart.
Masters of illusion. Their trade. 'We have trade
labels to suit every taste.' But, at the end of the day,
the only ones such trade truly benefits are their own …"

X

"Here all the oracles have fallen silent.
All the shrines have been abandoned. All
the chapels boarded up. The beloved
observances. The rituals and symbols
of centuries. Occluded. Mutilated.
The desert's getting nearer and
nearer." I watched my father as he
pondered us. Alienated sojourners. Worshippers
of false idols. He saw us straying
out of our dried-out paths into ruinous
ideological postures. Doctrinal, sentimental
utopias of political propriety. Thirsters
whom the thirst disfigures, distorts.

On our city walls and street corners
he saw only the graffiti of a corrupted
faith, of an ancient ceremony which,
dammed up, violently breaks out, asserting
itself. After he left I dreamed I saw him, and
his shabby contingent, again, walking
through the twilight dust of Uttarapath,
as if they were walking through a sacred
grove, far from what they'd experienced
here: rubble and spolia. Our chthonic
shrines long since dismantled and buried
beneath a network of motorways and malls.

XI

In the dead of winter, now, I return, to the
pitted granite of his headstone, tilting
on the small bluff above the river, as if
blown crooked by the wind which always blows
here. Beneath me, through thin aspen and alder,
the dust of a suburban Sahara moves on
the air in shadowy marsh light, darkening
against the edge of a sky grey as that half-
light moving up out of the river, and I know
there will not be another nekuia, that
'[we] will never find that life for which
[we] are looking.' A drowsy congregation,
laity of restless consumers, easily distracted
by each latest invention; deferential, mindlessly
concordant with our 'sowre complexion[ed]' clergy
in its towers of steel and glass, rising
above us. Victims of a corrosive insecurity,
we sail off into the future never looking
back; unable to ascertain, alienated
from repetition, a rhythm, a pattern, a music
woven into the air and the earth and
the heart which beats in accordance with it.

Notes

FIRE: acronym for the Finance, Insurance and Real Estate sector which accounts for most increases in wealth in modern Western capitalism.

House of Finance: the Mithraic remains are preserved in London within the basement of the headquarters of the American financial-data giant Bloomberg.

Turnpikes: Henry VII's 1489 act 'Agaynst the Pulling Doun of Touns'

Susie Campbell

Udder

What is ancestral in me knows as little as that skipping calf is oiled and clipped to bleed open the earth. Or is left wandering.

I was ready. But not for these, heads lowered and moving across my carpet at night, nostrils blowing with effort. Driven north across Europe: black as iron-gall, great vessels heavy with freight, stowaway calves hidden by their mothers' bulk. As a meteor leaves a glittering trail of horned gods, teats and cloven feet.

When you saw them on the hill, I blamed your failing sight. Floaters: residue close to the eye. Or the sun pooling in dips to distend the sides of shadows. But you insisted, *they're back*.

And so now they come. Always walking from left to right; a swollen matriarchy rolling hoof to implacable hoof, appearing and disappearing into the blank margin. Until it leaks its pale milk.

[Classification]

white precision of a point before burial mounds, tiny ivory-green
stars, past the bank where they grow. Nameless, low to the ground

spreading root

                beneath the earth a wild

what is at the door is not human. In her visions this stranger on the
flood, bells ringing over and grace springing up where the earth has
forgotten

           trail of white footprints   disturbs the
                    early   light

That solitary blue boat out there, who else would know she loved
tinned peaches, in my notebook this seems to be the best I can do:
water, a sign, whispering voices, then the damp smell of the muddy
current as the river is disturbed, drifting acid-sharp in my nose.
Before these modern gods

           in   places
           wasted and disturbed
           by her footprints   searching

was the Virgin Mary or Mother god(dess) sent to (or diagnosed).
First for classification was her religious melancholia, hallucinations,
a simplifying of their monstrous appearance – (*Stellaria Media L.*) for

Carl Linnaeus (1707–1778), Swedish botanist. Any known illness or nervous trouble starts to stand in for others

first   stars, then

chickweed, identified. Once classified as *Alsine Media L.* but also known as stitchwort, white bird's wye, or winterweed in open woodlands. As they pass into flowers in this genus, things become more metaphorical

a white precision

her name for them was satinflower or skirt buttons, the most common weed on the planet: found in waste places, disturbed ground, they diminish to white petals offset against the green, 'star-like' from the Latin

stand in   for
the object of the   search

Natasha Sajé

on privacy

our neighbor again drives drunk
this time not over penstemon
crushing their bearded tongues

this time on the highway   crash
landing in the ICU

toes lost to gangrene   a gangly loping walk
and what part of his mind to
nothing to do nothing to do but drink

and then get into his big orange truck

his wife clipped on the phone
closes the conversation
I feel I am thrusting myself into

a thick arborvitae hedge
breathing its broken woody scent
peering through crinkled leaves

to the empty pint bottle of Popov glinting from the curb

privacy once meant *the lack of public significance*
an undesirable state
to no longer count or be counted

now from behind fences and walls
electronic and other

we choose to shield
embarrassment and pain

while in moist November soil
the penstemon seeds itself
around shards of glass

at the Ouroboros Hotel

your story starts with a helicopter in from dragon peak and distant
sound of waves flute pristine knoll linen unfurled in breeze sunrise
the open front overlooking the lake in harmony with bird song Zeus
would feel at home cool water from fluted shells pointed amphorae
a bay curved and shiny as a scimitar sand soft as pillows beneath
bare feet a piping hot sauna northern lights beds covered with
cashmere moss paths burnished lenga beechwood mahogany teak
mineral rich syrah in the marble floored baths the goldleaf ballroom
surrounded by monkey puzzle trees a lobster picnic in a berber tent
under a grass thatched parasol on a pontoon at twilight hundreds of
flickering candles rose pink sandstone tiny lizards scattering balsam
jasmine scent walls hung with silk painted by hand cosseted by
moonlight meridians aligned stacked warm towels after the infinity
pool childhood state of being looked after happy as Aphrodite in the
clouds lapping this tale in your mouth

ashes of roses

I.
no one wears it today this Victorian shade
with more than a hint of mourning   more than a hint of love
petals and rock face clad in moon
white heat in cinders of extinguished fires
a semi-precious stone occluded
morganite perhaps unlikely turquoise
nuance of odd blend and whir
this cousin of regret   this mute and lighter form of ill
corolla of sweetness with an edible petiole

II.
of all which passed the feeling only stays
of a cap knitted for me by my godmother
in angora the soft pink rim and lamb's wool the gray rest
a thing of animal for animal
my baby head captived
so that a lifetime later I recall
unlike so much else   its inevitable necessity
not opaque to me like the future
not at all in shadow

Lucy Sheerman

Dearest,

That memory, let's not mention it, so much misunderstanding, layer upon layer, enough to fill a lifetime. How each sheet rustles like tissue paper, so fine a breath might disturb them. They do press down so upon your chest. Is this how you get to Hurt? Cocooned in a silence that holds the world at bay. I am making a border all around me, but it is filled with gaps; light and sound seep through. The walls are paper thin after all. Will you tell me now you love me? Send me a letter? Perhaps though I will not hear you out. Forgive me, I only want to imagine a room full of windows, vistas which stretch out the limits of this place. You won't tell me again, I suppose. See if I care or stoop to find the little phrases that spin across the floor, kicked into corners, apparently irretrievable.

Yours,

Dearest,

Sleep now. The walk was short but it was long enough. It takes time to recover. Day by day you may claw back more minutes (all except those lost ones, all that time we waited). It will be as if nothing is missed. We can make it so. I trace my path along this coast with all its histories of loss and forgetting and find I disappear almost as soon as the walk is over, only the scent of pine or sea lingers for a few moments. The dream that woke me is just a reminder of difference in scale. The house shrunk and all its beds discarded, a mangle, a gramophone and my shrill ingratitude all that is left. The dream and the creaking of a strange house, my companion's breathing and the glow of the unfamiliar kept me awake. Conscious of my place in the darkness at last, I was getting ready to leave. How lost I was, between countries and times and a sense of belonging. All this story will be a dream soon, and you dear reader, a fellow sleeper. The old, real life is the one that seems dreamlike, free of these new threats. Like these geese afloat on the freezing water, disturbed by the sudden sharp crack of gunfire, we see them flying into that bright sky, reflections skimming the water. Delicious irony, I might think, as we duck into the sanctuary of the house.

Yours,

Dearest,

I am creeping along these hallways like a wraith, unsure of my place. I am held by force of habit, the rhythm of each day shapes my path. My casting of shadows is so slight as to be imperceptible. I have to remind myself of that. The faintest pencil line, lost in the dense tracings already there, a hairline fracture, barely visible. I am clinging to the walls of this house like cloud. This cold spell transitory, the fog will lift and drift back out to sea. Each time I venture outside I hear the ducks, they counterfeit a forlorn chorus on cold and sociability. The sea air is healthful they say.

Here on this day without shadows, rocks and waves and tide drag the gaze back to that unburdening of sky into sea. This one is important, I try to set it aside, folded in a sheet of paper, but it slips from my grasp and suddenly they are all scattered. Is it better to love in the moment, letting it seize you painfully by the throat, or to remain waiting by the window and watching? Wait, listen to the footsteps that pace around this house. Watch as the light falls and the room goes dim again.

Yours,

Julie Mellor

Unwin Street

When I see our house in the photograph it's 1976.
The cousins from Canada have just arrived
and are squinting at our sun.
They chew gum endlessly and say *I guess*
instead of saying yes or no.
My mother has just finished cleaning the bay window.
Her hair's still in rollers.
In the street, the tarmac's melting
and Julie Fretwell's Afghan Hound is lying in the road.
We're posed with the cousins in height order.
They're all taller than us.
Dad is missing. He's up the drive, tinkering
with the engine of his hand-built speed boat
which he's painted orange and stencilled
with the name *Wild Oats*.

                    After tea, my mother says
no one's going anywhere without a life jacket,
but my brother doesn't want to go at all
because a packet of resistors has arrived
from Maplins so he can finish his hi-fi.
Due to the drought, the bath has to be emptied
with a washing up bowl. The water is carried
downstairs and tipped on the roses.
The roses aren't in the photograph.
Neither are the presents they brought us,
a key ring from the CN Tower in Toronto
and a fringed satin cushion that we slide off
every time we sit down.

Saga

In the Icelandic film *Rams*, two brothers who haven't spoken in
40 years end up in a blizzard. One is lulled to sleep by the cold.
The other digs a shelter, strips his brother to the waist, strips himself
and gives away his body heat. There are horses and dogs in the film,
but the focus is sheep. The brothers are shepherds. Each plays God
in a place where land is poor and the acid soil grows coarse grass.
When an outbreak of scrapie strikes, the government calculates each
man's worth in dead animals. The older brother pre-empts the cull
by slaughtering his flock before the vets arrive. The other appears
resigned, lets the killing proceed, but he's the one who hides his prize
ram in the cellar, along with enough ewes to start again. If this was a
metaphor for survival, the film would end here.

Weekend

Inside, caulked in the smell of new plaster
and drying paint, we wait it out.

You say what's important and I pretend to listen.
Really I'm listening to the hands of the rain

drumming their fingers on the new Velux.
Liberace, I think to myself.

Liberace never played so brazenly as this.
Condensation obscures what's left of the night.

We put the cork back in the bottle.
Someone is singing out there

like in films of rain where people don't care
that their socks are wet

and the cardboard that patches the holes
in their shoes is disintegrating.

The Exam

Part of him is here, entering the exam hall,
rows of iron-legged desks, tall windows
that let in the sounds of the city:
car horns, clarinets, hysterical women,

and part of him, albeit illusory
but certainly important to the narrative,
is idling on the narrow bed,
kettle boiling fitfully, three pairs of socks
soaking in a pink plastic bowl,

and what he believed was fog, earlier,
when he was only half awake,
is the street cleaners in their tin can trucks,
damping down the Paris dust.

Gillian Kidd Osborne

Sexual Dependency

Ever since my mother told me of the reproductive dependencies
of ivies, I've looked for them, the naked men among them,
 green, green, only that deep shiny jagged green, licked
with winter. And I've noticed, too, the separation gardeners
sometimes impose, casting the male corner-wise, away
from a row of showy red-flecked females, fruiting their display.

What's hidden and what's revealed?

When I ask you, What's invisible and what's revealed, that's
meant to be a sort of stage direction for an unimaginable play
you must imagine the players in the fray of an empty stage
as in a room of others a gorgeous aging poet asked, and
you must also imagine her gender, or her body otherwise
so braceleted and rigorously black. In consequence,

examining the brute elegance of

dependencies I have been taught to call women, recognize
as men. Torn acorns pocking the earth. Azaleas, evergreens
tucking their buds. If only you knew, mother Nature, how little
you have ever been a proper mother, over by the compost
regularizing love and decay. When a girl, I made my body
flower at the flower-market all purple with mudded hands

all those lovers, all those green

things, a man I might have loved, meanwhile my lover of
then, as if an overly kept bouquet or only a magnolia in the
way of things, shedding indecorous pink, how changeable he
was, predictable his changes as once were seasons, as after
wards when I was alone again the night trees smelling of
semen could I ever leave him I didn't think then that I would.

Allegory

For years, I wrote poems as a way of arguing with men. Then I stopped writing poems. Or stopped arguing. I don't remember which first. When argument left me, the departure was brutal, like a death, but in the background, a body silently dropping from a cliff to the rocks, while here, in the foreground, I became gradually more attentive to the bougainvillea, the robins that no longer went—where did they ever go?—in the coldest months. Other days, I read and sulked. I wasn't especially memorable or good. Life had become a frozen room.

> Once, Argument said he loved me.
> He had a wicked voice sometimes.
> Other days, soft as a goat's.

To return to this: the end of argument. I could say, the necessity of arguing with men ended when the right man let himself in, like a poem. But that would be to return to an inviting fallacy, of language's ameliorating magic in the thick wreckage of an otherwise orderly life, of the dumb fix of a woman's love for a reasonable man. When in Reality, there's a roughness in openness that wants surrender. There's a light at midday that desires pure smut.

> Once, Argument laid down his instruments
> so almost comfortably beside me that,
> but for bulk that inhibits all presence,
> our care for each other seemed almost

> > conversational. Taste = salt. Still,
> > it was the mastery of the grand gesture
> > that kept us that I couldn't abide.

Fever of Unknown Origin

On the thirty-seventh day of my sickness, this poem,
belatedly. I sat up in bed. As one does. When jostled

by terror. Terror was not as I was taught. Rather,
marginal, like a blender in a kitchen, a night-

light, some thing I had to look out for
on the way to a purpose. There it was. There, there.

Meanwhile, my body leached unknown illness
out the back of calves, wherever muscle

met sheet, a wet mark. Though they were with me
in the sickroom I was alone in the fever-room

reverberating, with mechanization's chords, near
        and out there. I wanted

                to read but I couldn't follow *The Ambassador's*
                        insinuating sentences. I wanted a friend
                but it was the worst time of night for companionship.
                                                        I wanted
                water. I wanted a daughter. I wanted palliative
                        care but first there was another
                                test. I wanted to rush but I was

still, the fever, like the poem, was parasitic, not entirely itself.
It lay bathed in night-lights like a person, shadow-weighted-
                                                        self.

99.9

Before I was sick I thought about sickness grammatically:
illness, present progressive, unwieldy ongoing verb.

Now I am running along the bike path now I am running
to catch the shuttle-bus now I am running a run in these
stockings now I am running a business now I am running
a racket now I am running a ponzi scheme now I am no
longer running now I am consigned to my bed now I am
running a fever every day for a day a week a month and

so on. Before I was sick I thought illness was like writing
in real-time, a pre-word-processing frenzy of papered ink.

Now, sickly, I see sick-time is slower than all that, slower
than linguistic activity. There's wall-watching in sickness.
But it wasn't a verb, or if it was, passive, the walls
happened to me, watched, past tense running up.

Ralph Hawkins

Toledo

the arrhythmic
breathing of
the snipe's
tiny heart
buttercups, poppies,
leading the way
up a beaten track
out of breath
coloured in pastels
& here is El Greco
a little box full
confined
of almond candies
breathe in Spanish
and sigh in Italian
passa 'l sospiro ch'esce del mio core
their painted hair and
fingernails dyed red

The Shape of Water

cycle of
in a field
rain drops
a drip
from a grey
tank
across an ocean
cuttlefish
the pink moons
of octopods

the th
ink of which
on the window
glass rain
hammers
pianoforte

pneuma

caged birds
possibly talking about the vet

discharge papers

fluffy synthetics with
a blow-up penis

it's pneumonia he said
not milk fever

those poor parakeets
colour coded

puffer jackets
detention centres

learning a new language

I hope she pecks off
his finger

From Jean-François Millet,
The Angelus & Robert Grenier

'from the trees in the woods'
a faint *cork* or *cark*
of birds

a dog by the hut rhymes
bark with bark

overhead the music
from the distant bell
the faint sound
of the evening angelus

a single rook
takes off
from the house
black against the light
of a tree

two in a potato field
and a crow contemplate

more birds in a
brass copper sky,
alight on the distant trees

free in the air

Out of focus

things to worry about

1 clowning
2 worm flu, rose
3 O holes
4 genetic mutation
5 boredom
6 bad poetry

gun tootin cowboys

circus knife throwers

how in town and city

containers into docks

kitchenware from the far
Far East winds

mice cats balloons and dogs

paid a fig roll
played a fig role

medication desired

Guy Birchard

Selections from ONLY SEEMLY

Thomas Burchard, labouring man, wife and six children, ex-Fairstead, Essex, aboard *Truelove*, Captain John Gibbs, master, bound for Massachusetts Bay, September, 1635. Zacharia Whitman, wife and junior.

Vivid, notwithstanding what never can have been lived. Sandhills adder, viviparous, brooding her clutch of eggs.

Lord appeared, black fedora, paunchy in gray suit, waddling along Dorchester, smoking a cigar, *Gazette*, could be *Star* (*Le Devoir?*) under left arm, lunchbag in right hand. Three layers of chin. Stately, seraphic. Montréal from just within the first portal into paradise.

Heading for the Sahara, there but to turn back. In idleness in Tagounit, full enough of the infamous White Cookie of Marrakech to foresee a quarter mile from town the silver dirham lost that long ago it lay not on but embedded in the hardpan.

Only later to kip vagrant in Cherbourg jail, whence ejected unbooked into dawn chill, sick.

Vancouver beerjerk on the hero-shift witnessed his VPD plainclothes regular stagger out pie-eyed one midnight, then return haggard first thing next morning, relieved nobody had dared pinch his wallet conspicuously mislaid on the banquette. Worst scenario averted: lost Badge found.

(for David Miller) Artless Canadian fails to stoop to clear the lintel of Berkshire inn yclept *The Jack Russell*, knocks his noggin. *So who was this J.R. feller? No person, sir*, publican deigns, *rather a fine breed of* terrier. *Ahh! pardon my naiveté. I'm* American, *you understand…*

Be Madigan's back-bar clock's tick soever audible, entertain such a pixilated notion as to learn to say – Irish! To which end, meekly drop the knocker on the Gaelic League's door. Only to have the oak slammed on yez for a *fekin' brazen amadán yank muppet*, all rendered in jackeen ire of mystifying origin.

Red fox, dissembling like a celebrity in shades and hat beset by autograph hounds, passing for a brindle calf, transformed in dudgeon and fled.

(for Merrill Gilfillan) Step onto the rear gangway, perigee moon caroming off Sunset Limited rails maken tracks outta Nawlins west of Lake Charles, east Texas way… Big Yellow Moonful. Immersion course in Spiritual.

Peaceless. Celestial elder, downcañon in Arroyo Seco seclusion, broke not his stride, only shifted his grip on his staff when he saw himself seen. No ebb, no faze. Ease, awe, sangfroid. Knowing who would the victor be.

Hollow rock polysibilance. Receding beach shingle sucked Straitwards by maximal calibre surf suspires at optimal tidal reach. *Hope holds up Despair's train.*

United Cigars de Campos: *Savoury exhalation points the Way — life's simple pleasure. Reflect upon Smoke while yet ye may…*

Death is tired. A scant metre from the mark, Death sits, head in hands, scythe at his feet. Life, fled before him so far so long, sits too, head hanging. Each catches his breath. Death is wry. Life approaches. Death's jaw drops.

The minuscule frayed puncture a .22 makes in target paper's black bulls eye: not visible without a spotting scope. Readers, as gods, at twenty-yard remove from *Hecatomb?*

Poetry persists, the recuperable poem soon gone. *Page 100.*

Think. All our Being may intend is in the event and disclosure of startling, temporal incidents, singular.

The last spear side Quaker, retired orchardist, hand banjaxed by virtue of boyhood transgression— *chopping wood on the Sabbath*—severe octogenarian

in fedora, three-piece suit and work boots, rolled a
mobile grindstone around the neighbourhoods of
the town at the service of the housewives' knives.

Note:
These selections from the 100 sections of *Only Seemly*, codicil to *Hecatomb*,
(Brooklyn: Pressed Wafer, 2017), comprise diverse matters of threshold
consciousness, profane *Moments, Bright* or *Stolen*, "re-enacted desire"
recouped with scalpel, magnifying glass, tweezers: what you alone see, or
sense, *that no one else does*.

Judita Vaičiūnaitė

translated by Rimas Uzgiris

Anapaestic

1.
Let me hear again the insomniac lark that sings
from the scent of lilacs blossoming blue, through foggy nights
when the balcony over the town becomes a stage
like the endless horizon of dawn – please don't take from me
this sleepless world where the pale and intricate stars
still fill the heart with light in a sacred hour of solitude
when the waking city enlarges the sky in a violet haze,
or when water murmurs under the bridges in ice-free streams.

2.
Ancient calendars with layouts of Vilnius's historic streets,
ancient calendars with brazen clocks of the dead marking time,
the ivies a century old, the courtyard's arch wound in thin
spiderweb speech, blocking you off from home,
where on my table a pile of faded notes grows,
all used and forgotten beside the telephones that no longer hear,
and the empty address books – I'm afraid of your murmur,
for the bloody past is turned into strophes under skies
bound up with fog, their memory fills – until one bitter day
amber leaves will fall on caryatids dozing away.

3.
Let the seasons change like chrysanthemums in a vase,
now turning brown, as their soft undulations appear in a barber shop
mirror,
and the face which you left in the dark as the trolley bus groaned
its meandering tread through the starless and soulless night of
November's sterility –
with your hair in the barber shop mirror again, let your sadness fall
with it too,
forget once more how a hopeless anxiety hounds us day after day,

and embrace the chrysanthemum's charming weave, why wait?
The pedestrians, streets, and cities still swarm –
these are the visions of the mirror of twilight's barber shop.

4.
It's the thaw's living water – just celesta, celesta, celesta I hear,
with the light that drips into my brain from the snowy window,
it's forbidden to be silent here like a marble mask on the wall,
we're allowed to sing naturally, in a joy without struggle, pure –
I can see the unfolding blossoms of begonias on fire in a vase
on a sill, made of clay, with the scent of the earth, in the middle of
the day –
but the sun of the thaw still sparkles cold and pale over the city,
in the balcony doors, the rays of the sun are like ivy winding around.

Untitled 1

The yellow-blooming mustard field.
    Oneness and sun.
A mood –
    like the turning of a hurdy-gurdy.
Edges grow dull,
    and in the warm, round world
something else,
    clear and weighty,
    climbs my throat.
Bitter yellow distances…
    I'm waiting for a miracle,
vainly trying to forget
    yesterday and myself.
All that's left is the rolling mustard sun –
    a state of weightlessness –
and love, giving me the meaning
    of tears and wind…

Untitled 2

I freeze like a pillar of salt,
stunned,
in front of my crumbling Old Town –
where a house burns
overgrown with frozen vines:
calligraphic characters under icy windows
crack off eaves and fall…

A hot, fetid backdraught
cuts through the sidestreet.
It accompanies a company of soldiers
headed to the sauna, a red light wavering in the leader's hand.
The smell of sweat returns. I gather voices and shadows,
forced to thaw out.

Untitled 3

A heart beats below the ice –
        Prussian, Livonian, Etruscan.
My pillow is wet with tears –
        come back, like the continuous cloud
of dust that follows marching armies,
        and look, with salty sea glare
into my heart,
        and speak – maybe
the pallid forms will move on a shield,
        or on broken vase…
        Because no one
ever dies – we are only oppressed
        by the filthy snow of thaws.

Air Raid

Pompeo Girolamo Batoni's *The Penitent Magdalene*, bombed by
British-American forces while in a wagon of paintings on a
Dresden street, February, 1945. From the history of paintings...

Mary Magdalene,
    fair-haired, gentle sinner,
Mary Magdalene,
    wearing classicism's mantle of unearthly blue,
Mary Magdalene,
    with an open, dusty book of prayer
    resting on a skull at night,
Mary Magdalene,
    painted with oils in a sunny master's studio,
Mary Magdalene,
    half-naked among sputtering candle flames,
Mary Magdalene,
    fondled by monks, thieves and Roman electors,
Mary Magdalene,
    letting down your long-gone hair like the rays of the sun,
Mary Magdalene,
    from the bomb-shelter –
    that bottomless cellar of brotherhood,
Mary Magdalene,
    from the drunken haunts of blood-stained soldiers,
Mary Magdalene,
    a starving recluse
    in 20th century libraries,
Mary Magdalene,
    tortured in the ghetto, the gestapo HQ
    or in a concentration camp,
Mary Magdalene,
    losing your form – becoming soul,
Mary Magdalene,
    redeeming sins beneath airplane wings,
Mary Magdalene,
    on a burnt-out Dresden street,
    forgive us,
    hear us,
    have mercy on us...

Under Electra's Virginal Statue

Under Electra's virginal statue
　　above the city sunk into gloom,
the river freezes, blended with night,
　　between December's banks –
winter stings the street,
　　even smiles go out – yet, continually patient,
with flurries above the frozen river's crook,
　　you plumb the depths
under Electra's light
　　where the Neris runs by the hospital pane –
it's already winter – you grasp at life now
　　like a pulsing vein.

Concert

Vivaldi and the breeze, the breeze, the breeze,
it's only the breeze of the evening growing rosy,

only the darkening park, before the fall of dew,
and the symphony playing on a terrace by the blue

sea, only clouds, streaming to the eerie light,
it's only five flapping ducks in wild flight,

only gulls and swallows swiftly leaving ardent
marks of shade like lacquer on the rose garden,

and the bird calls fall on the largo that fades away,
leaving only murmuring waves, only candles in bay

windows, blossoms crumbling, and summer closed
by pain, by only, and already, the scent of wilting roses.

Giedrė Kazlauskaitė

translated by **Rimas Uzgiris**

Silentium

Nothing dramatic happened – you didn't change your status,
didn't reply to the current discussion, didn't carry a banner
through the streets, and you didn't become a hero on glossy magazines
(though the effects aren't hard to achieve, inhumanly vulgar as they are).
You just lived, slowly, what others do not understand, from the perspective,
it seems, of an insufferable life when you wake up from a nightmare
screaming in the dark: they have released the guard dog –
symbolizing what is always hidden,
the ability to bite so many in the throat.

There was a revolution in Ukraine, social webs were buzzing
and all the personal video uploads looked like misery.
People got married with barricades in the background
and walked with mirrors against Berkut; our child was late to speak
so we dragged her off to the doctors who could tell us nothing
but that one must have hope.
Instead, she recognized the letters of her name
on the TV screen, and then, on the washing machine: joyfully
pronouncing each one, she enunciated them as if in Japanese,
having learned, most probably, from free cartoons
on YouTube. We began to understand – she remains silent
to avoid saying what doesn't need to be said,
keeping our lives safe.

A cold winter. Elementary students were not allowed in school,
but we took her to kindergarten so that I could go
to the seminars from which I recall the view along roofs
to the Bernardines' cross: it looked like I could reach it with my hand
and tie myself to the steed of dreams. But a lethargy settled down on me,
as if I had gone nowhere for a decade, as if I hadn't even seen the city;
people looked different now, marked by progress,

but still dissonant under asymmetric
classical vaults. I was behind on my dissertation,
even my mother lost her faith, saying:
"What do you need those studies for?" And I would dream
of her discovering our life together – condemning it, demanding
divorce (separation), mourning, terror, and then our aggressive,
white guard dog would get free: he could really attack people,
and we needed to hide to avoid the butchery.

Even though we lived in a cave (the catacomb figure is too high),
we would see the true letters of our names
in the shadow theatre of Maidan, but we remained silent
because of the dog.

Dolls from Guatemala

Two women with children – a girl and
a baby swaddled the old way; a wicker
cradle to rock him in, rolling-pin, broom,
a wicker basket for gathering goods, and
something similar to an oar.

We live like that too – in a half-
natural economy, chronically departing
for international conferences.

At the edge of town – so as not to draw
too much attention; people are good to us here.
We hide under uncomely clothes. We track
the viaduct in summer to kindergarten,
watching out for trains.

Their clangour unwittingly washes over us
with the rhythm of copulation, in dreams
this means a journey in one direction – death.

All kinds of things are written on trains,
especially in childhood, at least in thought.

So much nature here – we pick flowers
and medicinal herbs; nettles, dandelions, bishop's weed,
yellow stars from under the tracks.

I would have loved to have lived in dreams –
I invented so much in them,
what could not be reproduced in reality.

Hand-made dolls – I bought them
in Washington's Museum of the American Indian,
fearing extinction.

Indrė Valantinaitė

translated by Rimas Uzgiris

All the Rooms

All the rooms that have heard my laughter –
the backs of chairs, the closets whose darkness
sheltered my clothes when I was left white-bodied,
shining on my way to the bath,

wherein my weak little voice
would chase the latest tunes.

All the hotel soaps and towels
that washed and dried my tingling skin,

all the mattresses and springs that felt the weight of our love,

all the pillows in whose down my dreams were hid,

every mirror that has drunk my image above the sink –
in those mornings when I rose with rheumy eyes
in those rooms where I opened them –

remind me: how young and graceless I was,
and how strangely lacking in gypsy blood.

I would like to visit those places again before the end,
to gather me/us together once more, piece by piece.

I would glue together that puzzle – scattered, now,
over the seas and deserts of a fractured world.

In the Park

In the park, whose pond drowned bastard children,
whose branches broke under over-ripe lovers,
whose gates were wrought with unicorns making love,
our meandering shadow wrote the letter M.

Outsmarting the drunken guard, we waited for the gate's creak,
and the key that would waltz around the lock.

We had a mission to save ourselves –
in one night, to overcome the park's fright,
the owl's cry, the full moon's eye.

Fresh lovers, we knew our power,
sculptures in the nave of sighing boughs.

We kissed the greenhouse flowers out of thirst,
and as the fountain's water mirrored a dense
curtain of evening clouds, and the sun's face
dove behind the trees and church towers,

we became one like the booty in the belly of a whale.

I Will Be a Wolf

You brush your tongue
over my crooked front teeth,
passing the bridge with bandy boards
and on to the heart, two days by coach.

But I will be a wolf.
A courtesan's emery board.
A poisoned chalice.
A broken lock.
An invalid ticket.
A scratched record.
A shredded book.

I will attack your coach,
eating you alive –
so that you don't reach your destination
to drown me in bitter drops of inspiration.

Notes on Contributors

MARTIN ANDERSON has several collections with Shearsman, most recently the chapbook, *In the Empire of Chimeras* (2018).

JAMES BELL is Scottish and now lives in Brittany where he contributes photography and non-fiction to an English language journal. He has two previous poetry collections: *the just vanish space* and *fishing for beginners*, both from Tall-Lighthouse. He is currently at work on a first short-story collection.

GUY BIRCHARD – loafer at the sedentary trade: lay poet. Latterly of Victoria, British Columbia. Scholar of nothing. No degrees. No prizes. Neither profession, trade nor career. Anglo-Canadian. *Only Seemly* is in production at Pedlar Press (St. John's, Newfoundland) for autumn publication, 2018. Shearsman Books published *Aggregate: retrospective* in the Spring of 2018.

SUSIE CAMPBELL's poetry has been published in two chapbooks, *The Bitters* (Dancing Girl Press, 2014) and *The Frock Enquiry* (Annexe, 2015) as well as in a number of UK and international journals including *Shearsman, Long Poem Magazine, 3AM, Zarf* and *Cordite: The Mathematics Issue*. Her work has been included in Avant-Garde Visual Poetry Exhibitions 2017 and 2018 (Museum of Futures), and she created new work for the 2018 Poem Brut series, curated by S.J. Fowler. She is currently poet-in-residence for the 2017-2018 Mellon-Sawyer Post-War Commemoration series, jointly hosted by University of Oxford and Oxford Brookes University.

MARTIN CORLESS-SMITH was born in Worcestershire, and studied painting before moving to the USA, where he attended the University of Iowa Writer's Workshop and gained a Ph.D at the University of Utah. He teaches on the programme at Boise State University and edits the *Free Poetry* imprint. His next collection, *The Fool & The Bee*, will be published by Shearsman Books in early 2019.

CATHY DREYER Cathy Dreyer is a poet and critic who lives near Wantage in Oxfordshire. Her examination of Carrie Etter's *Imagined Sons* and Ted Hughes's *Birthday Letters* is shortly to appear in a special edition of Intellect's *Journal of Writing in Creative Practice*.

CARRIE ETTER is a frequent presence in these pages. Her fourth collection, *The Weather in Normal* is due from Seren in the UK and Station Hill Press in the USA. Her most recent Shearsman publication is the chapbook, *Scar* (2016), the text of which appears in the new book.

KHALED HAKIM lives in London. He has been absent from the poetry world for many years and is now making a return, with a book, *Letters from the Takeaway*, in development at Shearsman.

RALPH HAWKINS has three books from Shearsman and many more prior to that. The most recent is *It Looks Like an Island But Sails Away* (Shearsman Books, 2015).

JILL JONES was born in Sydney and has lived in Adelaide since 2008. She has published ten full-length poetry books and a number of chapbooks, including *The Beautiful Anxiety*, which won the Victorian Premier's Literary Award for Poetry in 2015, and Breaking the Days, which won the Whitmore Press Manuscript Prize in 2014 and was shortlisted for the Kenneth Slessor Poetry Prize in 2017. She has also won the Kenneth Slessor Poetry Prize and the Mary Gilmore Award. She has worked as a film reviewer, journalist, book editor and arts administrator. In 2014 she was poet-in-residence at Stockholm University. She currently teaches at the University of Adelaide where she is also a member of the J.M. Coetzee Centre for Creative Practice. Her most recent collections are *Brink* (Five Islands Press, 2017), and *Viva the Real* (University of Queensland Press, 2018).

GIEDRĖ KAZLAUSKAITĖ (b. 1980) studied Lithuanian literature at Vilnius University. Her first book, *Bye-Bye School!* (2001) was prose, her second *Hetaera Songs* (2008) was poetry. For the latter she was awarded the Young Jotvingian Prize. Her third book, *Postils* (2009), written together with Father Julius Sasnauskas, presents a commentary on the gospels. Her fourth collection, *Las Meninas*, appeared in 2014 and won the Jurga Ivanauskaitė Prize. In 2016, her fifth collection, *Singerstraum*, won the Writer's Union Prize and the Most Creative Book of the Year Award. Since 2010, she has served as the editor of the weekly cultural periodical *Šiaurės Atėnai*.

JULIE MELLOR holds a Ph.D from Sheffield Hallam University. Her poems have appeared in various magazines including *Ambit, Magma, The North, The Rialto* and *Stand*. Her pamphlets, *Breathing Through Our Bones* (2012) and *Out of the Weather* (2017) are published by Smith|Doorstop. She blogs at http://juliemellorpoetsite.wordpress.com

DREW MILNE's collected poems, *In Darkest Capital* came out from Carcanet Press, UK in 2017. *Earthworks* is forthcoming from Equipage in 2018 and *Third Nature* is forthcoming from Dostoevsky Wannabe in 2019.

DR. LANCE NIZAMI, BSc MSc PhD (all U.Toronto) originated in Lancashire. He now lives in Palo Alto, California. He is an independent research scholar who has published in the fields of Hearing Research and, more recently, Cybernetics. For the past seven years, he has occupied his few moments of spare time with writing poetry. His 250 accepted poems are spread over more than 100 print journals. PDFs of some of his scientific papers and letters can be accessed on ResearchGate and on Academia.edu.

GILLIAN KIDD OSBORNE's poems have appeared in journals such as *The Threepenny Review, Volt*, and *Zyzzyva*, and she has written essays and reviews for *The Boston Review, The Critical Flame, The New Inquiry, Nautilus* and other publications. With Angela Hume, she is co-editor of a collection of critical essays, *Ecopoetics: Essays in the Field*, and she is currently course manager and head teaching instructor for the Poetry in America course series at Harvard.

NATASHA SAJÉ is the author of three books of poems, most recently *Vivarium* (Tupelo, 2014); a book of poetry criticism (*Windows and Doors: A Poet Reads Literary Theory*, Michigan, 2014), and many essays. She teaches at Westminster College in Salt Lake City and in the Vermont College MFA in Writing program. www.natashasaje.com

HILDA SHEEHAN is Director of the Swindon Poetry Festival and has published a collection of poems, *The Night My Sister Went to Hollywood* (Cultured Llama, 2013), and two chapbooks from Dancing Girl Press, Chicago: *Frances and Martine* and *The God Baby* (with illustrations by Jill Carter).

LUCY SHEERMAN is currently working on a series of fan fiction treatments of iconic novels including *Rebecca* (Dancing Girl Press) and *Jane Eyre*. She was an artist in residence at Metal Peterborough where she co-created a new Evensong for Peterborough Cathedral which explored whether long term couples could take an extended journey to the moon together. Her sequence about the effect of the moon landings on the Apollo astronauts and their wives was published by Oystercatcher. Two plays, including a collaboration with the astronaut and poet Al Worden have been commissioned by Menagerie for the Hot Bed New Writing Festival.

ROBERT SHEPPARD's most recent book is *Twitters for a Lark* from Shearsman, a collaborative fictional poetry project to accompany his earlier *A Translated Man*. 'It's Nothing' is part of a long project of sonnets, part of which has appeared as pamphlets: *Petrarch 3* from Crater and *Hap* from Knives Forks and Spoons. He lives in Liverpool, and blogs at robertsheppard.blogspot.com.

JANET SUTHERLAND has three collections from Shearsman, the most recent of which is *Bone Monkey* (Shearsman, 2014). *Home Farm*, her fourth collection, will appear in early 2019.

BARBARA TOMASH is the author of four books of poetry: *PRE-* (Black Radish Books, 2018), *Arboreal* (Apogee, 2014), *Flying in Water* – which won the 2005 Winnow First Poetry Award – and *The Secret of White* (Spuyten Duyvil, 2009). Her poems have appeared in *Colorado Review, Denver Quarterly, Web Conjunctions, New American Writing, VOLT, Verse, Omni Verse, Witness, Hotel Amerika, Inter/rupture, Blaze/VOX, Bombay Gin* and numerous other journals. She lives in Berkeley, California, and teaches in the Creative Writing Department at San Francisco State University.

RIMAS UZGIRIS' poems and translations have been published in *Quiddity, Atlanta Review, Barrow Street, Hudson Review, AGNI, The Drunken Boat, The*

Massachusetts Review, Modern Poetry in Translation, Hayden's Ferry Review, The Iowa Review, Lituanus, Prime Number Magazine, inter | rupture, Presa Magazine, The Literary Bohemian, Literary Laundry, Brooklyner, Umbrella, Per Contra, and other journals. His book reviews have been published in *HTML Giant, Post Road, Words Without Borders* and *Rumpus*. His fiction appeared in *Writer's Abroad: Foreign Encounters Anthology*. He holds a Ph.D. in philosophy from the University of Wisconsin-Madison, and received an MFA in creative writing from Rutgers-Newark University. Recipient of a 2013 Fulbright Scholar Grant and a 2014 National Endowment for the Arts Literature Translation Fellowship, he teaches literature and creative writing at Vilnius University.

JUDITA VAIČIŪNAITĖ (1937–2001) – one of the most famous 20th century Lithuanian poets. Her first poetry book *Spring Watercolours* was published in 1960. She is the author of 20 poetry collections. Vaičiūnaitė also wrote poetry and fairy tales for children. "Vaičiūnaitė made Vilnius the locus of both Lithuanian poetic obsessions: nature and history. The city is not just any city. It is northern, yet Baroque. It is an occupied city, under Soviet rule, yet steeped in its own history and mythology of independence. And with this new emphasis on the urban came an unsentimental look at the life of a modern woman in the city: single, educated, working, struggling to be free", explains her translator Rimas Užgiris. *Vagabond Sun*, her selected poems in Uzgiris' English translation, is being published by Shearsman Books around the same time as the publication date of this issue.

INDRĖ VALANTINAITĖ (b. 1984), after graduating from a Jesuit high school, studied arts management at Vilnius University and at the Vilnius Academy of Arts. Her first book came out in 2006: *With Fish and Lilies*. It earned her first prize in the poetry category of the 2006 First Book Contest of the Lithuanian Writers' Union. Her second book, *On Love and Other Animals*, won the Young Jotvingian Prize in 2012. Her third collection, Short Films, appeared in 2017. In addition to writing poems, Indrė is a singer, winner of several singing festivals, and works as a TV journalist and producer.

TAMAR YOSELOFF is based in London; her most recent collection is *A Formula for Night: New and Selected Poems* (Seren, 2015). She is also the co-founder of Hercules Editions with designer and art editor Vici MacDonald.